A Commitment To Public Service

THE HISTORY OF
THE HOUSTON
BAR ASSOCIATION

A Commitment To Public Service

THE HISTORY OF THE HOUSTON BAR ASSOCIATION

Eric L. Fredrickson

A Project of the
Houston Bar Association

Gulf Publishing Company
Houston, Texas

A Commitment to Public Service
The History of the Houston Bar Association

Gulf Publishing Company
Book Division
P.O. Box 2608☐Houston, Texas 77252-2608

10 9 8 7 6 5 4 3 2 1

Library of Congress Catalog Card Number: 92-070629

ISBN 0-88415-082-8

Printed in the United States of America

Contents

Stephen F. Austin responds to complaints about lawyers.
Colonization attracts legal talent to Texas. The Allen brothers promote Houston. Houston as a political center. Frontier
jurisprudence. Justice in the Texas capital. The log courthouse and jail. James Jones and John Quick face the gallows.
Circuit riders. Judge Peter W. Gray: Leader of the Houston
bar.

The Houston bar organizes. Judge Peter W. Gray is elected
president. Legal practice in a frontier town. Thomas H. Ball
and the Houston Ship Channel. Judge Samuel H. Brashear
challenges the political establishment and becomes mayor.
The "battle of the streets." Captain Baker saves the Rice
Institute. Violence and corruption in a growing city. The
December gunfight. Houston lawyers organize the Harris
County Bar Association. The Houston Business League

endorses Oran T. Holt for mayor. Special meeting in the office of Hamblen, Scott & Hamblen. Judge E. P. Hamblen is elected president of the Houston Bar Association. The HBA campaigns for a new county courthouse.

The Harris County Law Library. Changes in the legal profession. Ben S. Campbell runs for mayor. Houston's "Night of Violence." Judge Brashear sends a warning. Houston lawyers and the Great War. The Ku Klux Klan organizes in Houston. Four members of the bench and bar are alleged to be Klansmen. Legal aid for the indigent. Richard T. Fleming and the HBA's first publication: *The Bar Association Syllabus.* The HBA debates its role in the selection of judges. The HBA drafts a new constitution. David A. Simmons and the *Houston Bar Journal.* Practicing in a depressed economy. Houston's young lawyers form the Houston Junior Bar Association. Walter Montieth overestimates the bar. The Texas bar integrates. J. S. Bracewell: Founding father of the modern HBA. Women join the profession. The HBA joins the Inter-American Bar Association.

War comes to Houston. The *Houston Bar Bulletin.* Colonel Leon Jaworski and the War Crimes Trials. The Soldiers and Sailors Civil Relief Committee. David A. Simmons as president of the American Bar Association. Judge Joseph C. Hutcheson, Jr., helps the HBA establish Houston's first Legal Aid Clinic. The State Bar of Texas awards the HBA the Award of Merit for Outstanding Achievement. The Women's Section and the Women's Auxiliary to the HBA are established. Mrs. Wilminor M. Carl becomes the first woman to serve on the HBA Board of Directors. Mc-

Carthyism and Houston's "Red Scare." An anticommunist oath for lawyers. Electing the association president: The unwritten tradition. The George W. Ebey Affair. From association president to city mayor: Lewis W. Cutrer. Law Day, USA. Joyce Cox proposes a Houston Legal Center. Few lawyers share his vision. ". . . they say the Bar Association has no meaning."

CHAPTER FIVE
Expansion and Innovation, 1960–1972 104

The *Houston Bar Bulletin* becomes *The Houston Lawyer.* Developing programs that serve the community. New offices and an expanded staff. The HBA votes for desegregation. The significance of *Gideon v. Wainwright.* Tom Phillips: Architect of the Houston Legal Foundation. The local challenge to legal aid: *Touchy v. Houston Legal Foundation.* An award from the American Bar Association. Recommendations for a Family Law Center. Joyce Cox's vision fulfilled: The Houston Bar Center. The legal-aid funding crisis. The HBA celebrates its 100th anniversary at the Astroworld Hotel. The Saturday meeting at Quail Creek. Leon Jaworski serves as president of the American Bar Association.

CHAPTER SIX
A Mandate for Professionalism, 1973–1990 ... 139

Watergate renews public criticism of lawyers. Leon Jaworski as special prosecutor. The phenomenal growth of Continuing Legal Education. A judicial evaluation poll for Texas. Bracewell & Patterson challenges the unwritten tradition. "Operation Reachout." A new constitution for Texas— "Who Cares?" Alternative Dispute Resolution. The vision of James B. Sales. Restructuring Houston's legal-aid programs. Funding the administration of justice: The Houston Bar Foundation. The debate over judicial selection. "Lawyers Care": The administration of John J. Eikenburg. A new mandate for professionalism.

Acknowledgments

I wish to thank Dr. Martin Melosi, Director of the Institute for Public History, University of Houston, and Dr. Jack August for giving me the opportunity and scholarly guidance to do the Houston Bar Association history project. I am especially indebted to the Historical Committee of the Houston Bar Association for its enthusiastic cooperation and support in writing the history of the Houston Bar Association. It has been a distinct pleasure to work with successive committee chairs Clinton F. Morse, Charles W. Giraud, and Jeffrey D. Dunn. I am also indebted to Kay Sim, Executive Director of the Houston Bar Association. She always made me feel right at home whenever I visited the Association's office to conduct research. Above all, I wish to thank my wife, Dena M. Fredrickson, whose "happy talent for composition and remarkable felicity of expression" infused this manuscript with a degree of clarity which would otherwise have not been possible.

Foreword

A lawyer is an advisor, negotiator, advocate, and intermediary for clients, an officer of the courts, and a public citizen having special responsibility for the quality of justice. Lawyers, as guardians of the law, play a vital role in the preservation of our society. The Houston Bar Association, a voluntary organization of approximately 9,900 lawyers practicing in Houston and Harris County, has sought to promote the ideals of the legal profession for more than a century. This book is a chronology of the struggles and accomplishments of the HBA's past and its tradition of commitment to public service.

The HBA Board of Directors laid the foundation for this book by creating the HBA Historical Committee in 1986. Committee members conducted interviews and gathered research sources that eventually led to a feasibility study for a comprehensive work. In 1989, the HBA contracted with the University of Houston, Institute for Public History, to write the manuscript. Eric Fredrickson, then a graduate student at that Institute, assumed the task with enthusiasm and perseverance.

Writing over a period of two years, interrupted by active service during the Persian Gulf War, Eric Fredrickson produced a narrative that weaves an impressive account. The history of the HBA mirrors the ups and downs of Houston's own development and progress. Mr. Fredrickson's work provides a perspective on the forces that helped transform Houston from a small frontier settlement to a modern, world-class city.

Houston Bar Association Historical Committee

Introduction

A visitor to Houston in 1879 wrote, "The city looks shabby. There is not a paved or macadamized street in the town, and but few decent sidewalks, and no system of sewers at all."[1] Historian George M. Fuermann attributed this state of disrepair to "the lingering effects of Reconstruction, an enfeebling and often corrupt phase of Houston's municipal government."[2] These conditions highlighted the problems facing Houston's lawyers when they organized the city's first formal bar association in April 1870.

Although there is insufficient evidence to support any definite conclusions about the impetus behind the 1870 Houston Bar Association, it is probable that Houston lawyers organized it to elevate the standards of the bar and present a unified front against Radical Reconstruction. Despite the lofty intentions of Houston's lawyers, the first Houston Bar Association, for reasons unknown, was short-lived. When Houston's second bar association, the Harris County Bar Association, appeared in December 1901, lawyers of the newly formed organization resolved to "weed out" the "shysters." The immediate catalyst for organizing was public outrage over an attorney's alleged involvement in the murder of two policemen. Like the 1870 bar association, the Harris County Bar Association was also short-lived. Two years later, however, Houston lawyers "finally found a purpose that could sustain a bar association." The present Houston Bar Association (HBA) was formed on March 26, 1904, to "cultivate a social spirit" among lawyers and to organize an annual dinner.[3]

The bar association movement in Houston and in other cities throughout the United States was a post–Civil War phenomenon. Galveston lawyers organized the first city bar association of that period in 1868. The Bar Association of the City of New York organized in February 1870, followed by the first Houston Bar Association in April the same year. Between 1870 and 1878, lawyers founded eight city and eight state bar associations in twelve states. In 1878, "seventy-five gentlemen from twenty-one jurisdictions" met in Saratoga, New York, to organize the American Bar Association. The Texas Bar Association organized in Galveston in 1882. By 1890, there were twenty state or territorial bar associations and at least 159 city or county bar associations.[4]

Historians generally have explained the bar association movement as "the legal profession's efforts to come to terms with a society that was rapidly becoming urbanized and middle class."[5] Legal historian Kermit Hall claims that bar associations were part of "the push toward professionalization and the growing social importance of lawyers." Elevating the standards of professional conduct was at the heart of the professionalization movement. "Leaders of the bar formed themselves into associations whose purpose was to encourage a sense of professional distinctiveness among fellow practitioners," asserts Hall.[6] However, neither the American Bar Association nor the state and local bar associations were truly representative of the entire bar. Early associations were primarily social clubs that made admission "dependent upon recommendation by current members and a screening process."[7]

According to Hall, the professionalization of law occurred "at the same time that other middle-class occupations such as engineering, medicine, and education were developing their own 'professional cultures.'"[8] But while engineering standards and medical standards were vital to ensuring a higher level of public safety and service, it was the legal profession that directly affected the very sinews of the nation's democratic heritage. A country of laws needed men and women trained in the law who were intellectually and morally fit to serve the public.

Bar associations functioned as a vehicle for regulating entrance to the rapidly growing legal profession and for maintaining high standards among practitioners. As legal scholar Richard Abel says,

"One can see the inspiration for these [bar associations] in the fact that three out of their five original committees were concerned with admissions, legal education, and grievances."[9]

The character of these bar associations varied from state to state and city to city, reflecting the particular needs of each community. As Houston grew and the legal and social needs of the community changed, so did the activities of its lawyers. The period 1870 to 1920 was characterized by city growth and the role of lawyers in that growth. Many of Houston's prominent lawyers were active in promoting and building Houston, and several of them served as mayor. Such men were both lawyers and civic boosters. "City building" was a major part of their lives. By 1920, Houston's growth and economic prominence was assured, and lawyers began focusing their activities on "advancing the science of jurisprudence" and offering services to the community.

Today the primary purpose of the Houston Bar Association is to serve its members and improve the administration of justice. Its secondary purpose is to serve the local community in the "spirit of public service."[10] The association's emphasis and approach in each area has varied and changed over time. From its original goal of "cultivating a social spirit," the association's function has become much broader. "It is inclusive now of civil rights, minority rights, the homeless, AIDS, legal services to indigents—it covers many aspects of our society," says Pearson Grimes, past president of the HBA.

The HBA's evolution from "social club" to champion of community services did not happen overnight and was dependent ultimately on the individual leadership and the willingness of members to give freely of their time and energy. As former HBA President Joe L. Draughn once said, "Volunteerism is the backbone of our association."[11] In any voluntary organization, it is the people that make the difference. An active membership and innovative leadership are the key to growth and success. "The bar president," said former HBA President Thomas M. Phillips, "can simply hold the office with whatever honors involved and show up at picture taking time, or he can attempt to utilize the short tenure he has to accomplish something."[12] The high points and major accomplishments of the HBA largely reflect the motivation and aspiration of its officers and the difference they tried to make.

When assessing the social significance of the HBA, it is important to consider the observation made by Joe Draughn in 1976: "An organization should not be judged simply by its longevity. Rather, its success should be measured by the extent to which it achieves its purpose for existing; and on a higher plane as to whether achieving that purpose contributes to the betterment of its members and the public which they serve."[13] The HBA continues to be an important vehicle for both professional and public services. Whereas it is difficult for a handful of attorneys to organize and sustain professional and community projects on a large scale, the HBA provides the resources and coordination necessary to galvanize lawyer volunteerism and produce positive results.

In 120 years, the HBA has grown from a fledgling organization of thirty-seven lawyers in a frontier town to the nation's sixth largest metropolitan bar association. This is the story of that growth.

CHAPTER ONE

The Early Days of Houston Jurisprudence, 1837–1869

Lawyers have played a role in the shaping of the Texan character from its earliest stirrings. As early as 1829, the Texas colonizer Stephen F. Austin declared, "An honest and conscientious lawyer is a valuable member of society—there is none more so—but a hot-headed, fractious and contentious lawyer is a curse on any community."[1] In Texas' colonial period as today, lawyers were a familiar target for criticism, with colonists complaining that lawyers' "manner of doing business" was to blame for the "difficulty" and "uneasiness" among the people in their daily transactions.[2] Upon hearing such criticism, Austin responded that lawyers were indeed a "great evil" but that it was the colonists themselves who encouraged such behavior. Austin placed blame for the increase in litigiousness on the American national character. The import of his remarks should not be lost on modern ears:

It is a part of the national character of Americans to be contentious and litigious, and I do believe that a lawyer would fatten on 100 Americans, when he would starve on 10,000 of

1

any other people on earth. If you wish to correct this evil therefore go to the foundation and cut it up by the roots. Let every man settle his differences by an arbitration of his neighbors, or if he goes to law let him attend to his own business and not employ a lawyer.[3]

Austin's response not only evidences that lawyers were present in Texas seven years before it became a republic but also illustrates, perhaps surprisingly, that the tension between the legal profession and society at large is not a recent phenomenon. The solution Austin recommended, neighborhood arbitration, is remarkable in that it predates the relatively recent development of its modern equivalent, alternate dispute resolution, by some 150 years.

Colonists flocked to Texas in the years before the Texas Revolution seeking opportunity and new lives. Lawyers were among those who settled Texas and fought for her independence; among the more prominent were Sam Houston, William Barret Travis, and David G. Burnet. Two of the new Republic's first jurists were Andrew Briscoe and Algernon P. Thompson. Andrew Briscoe came to Texas in 1833 with the intention of opening a law office, but he became a merchant instead. A staunch supporter of breaking ties with Mexico, Briscoe was one of the signers of the Texas Declaration of Independence. After commanding a company of Texans at the Battle of San Jacinto, Briscoe settled in Harrisburg; soon after, President Sam Houston appointed him chief justice of Harrisburg County. Algernon P. Thompson was born in England in 1818 and moved to New York sometime prior to November 21, 1835, when he entered the army of the provisional government of Texas as a second lieutenant. A veteran of the Battle of San Jacinto, Thompson became a successful Houston lawyer and judge after the Texas Revolution.[4]

When settlers migrated to the part of Texas that was to become the city of Houston, a unique blending of individualism and commitment to public service gave birth to a new community, animated from its inception by a spirit of free enterprise. On August 26, 1836, two New York speculators, the brothers Augustus C. Allen and John K. Allen, purchased two leagues of land on the banks of Buffalo Bayou for $5,000.[5] Named in honor of General Sam Houston, the new town was aggressively marketed by the Allen brothers, who claimed that

Houston's location "must ever command the trade of the largest and richest portion of Texas" and that "nature appears to have designated this place for the future seat of government."[6]

Although it was some time before Houston developed into a regional commercial center, the Allen brothers correctly predicted their town's political future. The first Congress of the Republic of Texas met in October 1836 at Columbia (now West Columbia) and two months later selected Houston as the republic's new capital. More importantly, Congress also designated Houston the new county seat of Harrisburg County (which became Harris County in December 1839).[7]

When President Sam Houston arrived in the new Texas capital in late January 1837, there was only "a small log cabin and twelve persons."[8] But the town grew rapidly as people immigrated "from all directions," and by March, Houston had a population of "some four or five hundred people."[9] One immigrant noted that Houston had "but one attorney," but that changed quickly as the town's political importance attracted lawyers. By fall the number of attorneys had "swelled to fifteen or twenty."[10]

During May 1837, advertisements appeared in the *Telegraph and Texas Register* announcing the formation of the law partnership of Thomas J. Gazley and John Birdsall, who also "propose[d] to connect with their professional business a Land Agency, for the purchase, location and sale of land, and the investigation of titles."[11] William Fairfax Gray, a Virginian who came to Texas in January 1836 and observed the proceedings of the Convention that declared Texas independence at Washington-on-the-Brazos in March 1836, also announced the opening of his law practice in Houston, promising that "deeds, powers of attorney, and other instruments of writing" would be "carefully and promptly drawn."[12] In June 1837 former *ad interim* Republic president David G. Burnet and Isaac N. Moreland announced their law partnership.[13]

In 1837, most Texas attorneys lived and practiced outside urban areas and the cases they handled were "an extremely miscellaneous lot, ranging from probate matters and divorces through contract and land actions to a broad spectrum of criminal prosecutions."[14] The officers of the court also varied in ability, and proceedings lacked uniformity. While visiting Brazoria in April 1837, William Fairfax

Gray noticed that the practicing lawyers and presiding judge were "mostly young men" and that the proceedings were "loose and not very ceremonious."[15] Available sources for legal research were virtually non-existent. Law books were a rarity for lawyers and judges practicing on the frontier. There were also few judicial precedents, and judges had little regard for what few precedents did exist. Texas courts reached their decisions by taking the facts of the case and testing them by the principles of equity.[16]

The Eleventh District Court for the Second Judicial District was organized in Houston on March 20, 1837, with Benjamin C. Franklin, Judge; James S. Holman, Clerk; and John W. Moore, Sheriff.[17] The grand jury brought in three indictments at its first session: Whitney Britton for assault and battery; John T. Beall for murder; and James Adams for larceny.[18] As there was no courthouse, the court convened under the open trees on Courthouse Square and the jury sat on logs and old crates.[19]

Britton plead guilty and was fined $5, the court taking consideration of "the exculpatory affidavits presented."[20] Deciding that Beall had done "no more than they would have done under the circumstances," the petit jury delivered a verdict of justifiable homicide. Adams, however, received "the full vigor of an outraged justice" and was convicted for theft. For having violated the sanctity of property, the court ordered Adams to return the stolen funds and papers and sentenced him to get "thirty-nine lashes on the bare back and be branded with the letter 'T' in the right hand."[21]

The man responsible for convicting Houston's criminals was Augustus M. Tomkins, the county's first district attorney. Although Tomkins was a hard-working public servant who "stood pretty near the head of the bar," his accomplishments were marred by what one contemporary described as "rather wild habits."[22] In a letter to President Mirabeau B. Lamar in February 1839, Andrew Briscoe, chief justice of Harrisburg County, complained that Tomkins was

a man destitute of all moral principle, a spendthrift, a gambler and a *debaucher,* or one in the habit of taking too much *steam* aboard—a man who has too many necessities for money to be always honest in the discharge of his official duties—a man who instead of aiding to execute the laws is known oftener to violate them than probably any other man in our country.[23]

Judge Briscoe also accused Tomkins of "dissipation and rioting," a characterization that the official court records confirm. While serving as district attorney, Tomkins's own court indicted him twice for assault and battery and convicted him on at least one count. After the expiration of his term as prosecutor in September 1839, Tomkins was fined in Harris County for carving on the courtroom furniture, indicted in Galveston County as an accessory to murder, and indicted in Travis County for assault and battery.[24]

The first public buildings erected in Houston were the county courthouse and the county jail. The courthouse was a double log cabin with the court in one room and the clerk's office in the other. Each room was sixteen feet square. Both the courthouse and jail were located on the Congress Avenue side of Courthouse Square, near the Fannin Street corner. The city's first jail was a rather crude structure made of logs. According to one contemporary, the jail

> had neither windows nor doors. It was simply a one-story log house with a flat roof. On its top was a trap door. This was raised, a ladder was lowered and the prisoner went down into the jail. Then the ladder was withdrawn, the trap closed, and the prisoner was left to meditate on his sins.[25]

By 1844, the condition of the log courthouse had deteriorated to such an extent that the county had to abandon it. Between 1844 and the completion of the county's first brick courthouse in 1851, judicial activities "were conducted in a variety of locations: T. B. J. Hadley's City Hotel, Schrimp's Hotel, and M. Cavanaugh's brick store at $25 per month."[26] Due to "poor material, faulty construction or some other cause," the county's second courthouse lasted only nine years.[27]

One of the newcomers to Houston was a young attorney from Kentucky named John Hunter Herndon. Herndon's first Texas stop was Galveston, where he embarked on the steamboat *Sam Houston,* which he described as "a small filthy, horribly managed concern," to travel the remaining seventy-five miles to Houston. Herndon's trip up Buffalo Bayou was not pleasant. Departing Galveston on January

19, 1838, the *Sam Houston* grounded on a sandbar after steaming seventeen miles. The crew and passengers spent the entire next day getting off the bar, only to have the boat ground again seventeen miles later. According to Herndon, many of the passengers were dissatisfied and some even spoke of wading ashore and walking the remaining forty-one miles to Houston. The *Sam Houston* finally arrived in Houston on January 23, and Herndon set out to establish a law practice.[28]

The Harrisburg County court term for Spring 1838 began on March 19 with Judge James W. Robinson presiding. Herndon was in attendance and described the courthouse as "a scene of constant confusion produced by the lawyers, clerks, and sheriffs." At this term of the district court, the grand jury brought in 120 indictments: for gambling, thirty-six; vending without license, twenty-seven; various crimes against property, eighteen; assault, fourteen; issuing change notes, ten; fornication, five; murder, four; high treason, one; charge unknown, five.[29]

Two of the men indicted for murder were James Jones and John Quick. Jones had killed a fellow soldier of the New Orleans Grays, and Quick had killed a man with whom he was gambling. Jones stood trial on Thursday, March 22. Despite defense counsel's attempt to "take advantage of legal technicalities and imperfections in pleadings," the jury quickly convicted Jones of murder. The following day the jury convicted Quick, who Herndon described as "a savage bloodthirsty, malicious looking devil, who changed not a feature or muscle of his face upon the verdict being announced."[30]

Judge Robinson overruled all motions for a new trial and set sentencing for March 24. In a last attempt to prevent sentencing, an unidentified party, hoping to elicit sympathy, informed the court that "the jail was very insecure, the weather quite cold and the men forced to wear irons for greater security because of the weakness of the palisade jail." Apparently touched by the party's plea, Judge Robinson pronounced sentence that Jones and Quick, "in consequence of the insecurity of the jail, the extreme cold weather and their uncomfortable situation," be hung on the following Wednesday between the hours of 6 and 2 p.m.[31]

On Wednesday, Herndon and "a concourse of from 2,000 to 3,000 persons" gathered in a clump of timber on the south edge of town to see Jones and Quick hang. While standing on the gallows, Quick "addressed the crowd in a stern, composed and hardened manner" while Jones "seemed frightened." Both men "swung off" the gallows at 2 p.m. and were cut down and pronounced dead thirty-five minutes later.[32]

The execution of Jones and Quick testifies to the promptness of justice within the Republic of Texas. According to one Texas lawman from those early days, "When [criminals] were proven guilty they were always hanged . . . there were no appeals in those days; no writs of errors; no attorney's fees; no pardon six months later. Punishment was swift, sure and certain."[33]

An integral component of the Texas judicial system was circuit riding. W. D. Wood has left a vivid description of what it was like for members of the bar to follow the judge on his circuit from county to county in the early 1850s:

> They traveled on horseback. Each had his saddle-bags (in which was stored his linen and generally a lunch), his blanket, lariat, tin cup, water gourd, and coffee pot. All of these accouterments were necessary. The country was thinly populated, and often in passing from one county seat to another no place of entertainment would be found, and camping out then became a necessity. When this happened, a spot affording water and grass was, if possible, selected for camp. Having chosen the place the travelers dismounted, unsaddled and staked their horses, kindled a fire, made and drank coffee, and ate their lunch. After eating and drinking, they sat around the camp fire, joked, told anecdotes, discussed the topics of the day, sang a song or two, and thus pleasantly whiled away the time till they grew sleepy, when they rolled themselves in their blankets, with saddle and saddle-bags for pillow, and with easy conscience passed into the land of dreams. These were the golden days of enjoyment and good fellowship. With every honest lawyer it was hail fellow well met. No envy or jealousy, no underbidding or struggle for fees.[34]

Peter W. Gray was one of those who spent time as a circuit rider in the early days of Texas jurisprudence. Gray served as Harris County district attorney in the early 1840s and represented the county in the first and fourth state legislatures. From 1854 until the outbreak of the Civil War, Gray served as judge of the Eleventh District Court.[35] As a district judge, Peter Gray "had to go from county to county on horseback, or in a buggy, or by stage—and plow through mud and swim overflowed creeks to keep his official engagements."[36]

Peter W. Gray was the son of William Fairfax Gray. William Fairfax Gray was the acknowledged leader of Houston's early bar and was serving as the district attorney at the time of his death, which resulted from "exposure to inclement weather in traveling horseback over the district," in 1841. Peter Gray followed in his father's footsteps, entering the bar in May 1840. As a young lawyer, he learned proper courtroom etiquette the hard way. While trying one case, the court fined him $20 for sitting on a table, and another $20 for smoking in the courtroom. Despite such fines in his early years, Gray did not "display his authority by entering fines against lawyers" when he was later a judge.[37]

After William Gray's death, President Sam Houston appointed Peter Gray to succeed his father as district attorney. In 1846 he served in the first state legislature where he "brought order out of chaos and light out of darkness" by writing the Practice Act of 1846, which established the basic ground rules of pleading and procedures in Texas courts. Chief Justice Roberts of the Texas Supreme Court characterized Gray as "the very best district judge that ever sat on the district bench of Texas."[38]

Gray possessed an excellent legal mind, and he never allowed the dignity of his court to be tarnished—even if it was threatened by someone outside his courtroom. During one trial, a local man with a reputation for public drunkenness stood in front of the courthouse and created a loud nuisance. After the man refused the Sheriff's request to quiet down, Judge Gray recessed the court and went outside to rectify the problem. On seeing Gray, the man brandished a pistol and said, "Judge Gray, I am on the public square where I have the right to be, and you have nothing to do with me, and you mustn't bother me." Ignoring the man's warning, Gray grabbed the man by the collar and led him into court, where Gray fined him $100 for contempt.[39]

Judge Peter Gray signed the Texas Secession Declaration and served in the Confederate Congress during the Civil War. After the war, Gray returned to Houston and resumed his practice of law, "endeavoring by example and counsel to reestablish the order of peaceful pursuits and ameliorate the condition of his people."[40] In 1865, Gray formed a law partnership with his cousin, Colonel Walter Browne Botts.[41]

The first Union soldiers marched into Houston on June 20, 1865.[42] The era of Reconstruction was about to begin. In these years following the Civil War, as the nation struggled to reunite itself, lawyers in Texas and throughout the country turned to professional organizations as a means of policing the profession and as a cohesive force through which to address mounting social and economic problems.

CHAPTER TWO

Organizing the Bar, 1870–1910

On a Saturday afternoon in April 1870, Houston's lawyers held a meeting at the newly remodeled courthouse to organize a bar association and elect officers. The Houston *Telegraph* reported that the chief objectives of the newly formed Houston Bar Association were "raising the standard of the legal profession, and the purchase of a law library."[1] And while charter members like bar president Peter W. Gray, Colonel John H. Manley, George Goldthwaite, and Colonel Walter Botts undoubtedly dedicated themselves to the accomplishment of these objectives, other pressing problems existed within the legal community and in local politics that helped galvanize Houston lawyers into joining the city's first bar association.

On the night of August 20, 1868, popular Houston attorney and political orator W. H. Crank was making a speech at a Democratic party meeting in the Fifth Ward. Crank narrowly escaped an attempt on his life when a would-be assassin fired a bullet into the branches overhanging the speaker's platform as Crank addressed the crowd. In the ensuing excitement, Crank's assailant made his escape and was never apprehended. Two days later, the Houston *Telegraph* condemned the attack and said that it was "a pity that such cowardly transgressors go unwhipped of justice."[2]

The attempt on Crank's life was indicative of Houston's troubled times as the Reconstruction Era came to a close. The postwar economy was in depression, and the city could not absorb the large influx of carpetbaggers and freed slaves who looked to Houston as a place of opportunity. Overcrowding and unemployment, together with corruption in local government, led to crime in the streets that went largely unchecked by the efforts of local law enforcement and was often exacerbated by "shady deals" by certain officers of the courts. When the city remodeled the county courthouse during the spring of 1870, a local paper criticized the effort by citing a lack of shade trees in the courthouse square: "Probably the authorities around it fancy that [the square] is already sufficiently *shady* to enable them to dispense with any additional adornment in the way of trees and shrubbery."³

At about the same time that Houston lawyers were organizing a bar association to address contemporary problems, concerned citizens organized a secret society whose objective was "to maintain the supremacy of the white men by lawful means and to restore law and order."⁴ Placing the blame for the increase in crime on supporters of Radical Reconstruction and freed slaves, this organization called itself the "Teutonic Band of Brothers," but some Houstonians believed that the group was in reality the Ku Klux Klan.⁵

The Teutonic Band of Brothers also targeted the proliferation of crime, and through its activities law and order eventually returned to Houston. Dr. S. O. Young, an early chronicler of Houston's history, joined this organization at the invitation of a young lawyer named Colonel Jones. According to Young, there were ten charter members, of which Colonel Jones was No. 1. Eventually more than 300 of Houston's leading citizens joined the secret society. Young stressed that the society "was an absolutely lawful organization."⁶

The Radicals even manipulated the judicial system by removing judges from their assigned cases for political reasons. In February 1868, Judge William Fayle presided over a trial in which an innocent child was accidentally shot to death when an argument between J. G. Tracy, editor of the pro-Radical newspaper the *Union,* and Sommers Kinney, editor of the Democratic *Times,* escalated into a gunfight. Newspaper accounts reported that Tracy had threatened to shoot Kinney on sight for the derogatory remarks Kinney had made about

him. Although Kinney tried to avoid Tracy, the two men unexpect-
edly met, and although neither man was injured, one of Tracy's shots
tragically killed a young boy. The authorities charged Tracy with
murder and scheduled him for trial in Judge Fayle's court. Before the
trial began, however, Major General J. J. Reynolds, military commander of Texas, removed Judge Fayle and appointed a Radical
sympathizer named Samuel Dodge in his place. As expected, Judge
Dodge acquitted Tracy of the murder charge and fined him a mere
$100 for aggravated assault. To Houston's civic leaders, the dismissal
of Judge Fayle and the acquittal of Tracy was a "clear perversion of
justice" and was typical of the partisan politics they found so hard to
swallow.[7]

The Houston legal community was also concerned about the
restructuring of state district courts upon Texas' readmission to the
Union in 1870. Certain provisions of the new constitution abolished
county courts and transferred all matters to the district courts. The
local bar feared that Radical Republican governor Edmund J. Davis
would pack the courts with appointees from his own party; the last
thing Houston attorneys wanted was more Radicals on the bench. It
is probable that this development, along with the memories of
Tracy's acquittal by a Radical puppet judge, prompted the lawyers
of Houston to organize in order to present a unified front against the
Radical Republicans. In one of its first official acts, the newly
formed Houston Bar Association succeeded in convincing Governor
Davis to appoint conservative democratic Judge James R. Masterson
to the Eleventh District Bench.[8] In so doing, the association was able
to strike a blow against Radical rule in the Texas courts. In studying
the Galveston Bar Association, formed just two years earlier, the
legal historian Maxwell Bloomfield concluded that the program of
Radical Reconstruction then going forward provided "a strong
impetus for bar organization."[9] Given Houston's proximity to
Galveston and the fact that lawyers from both cities often corre-
sponded or came face to face in the courtroom, it is understandable
that the political concerns of Galveston's lawyers were also the
concerns of Houston's lawyers.

In those days a colorful assortment of crime filled the court
dockets. One A. Balldina was fined $10 for drunk and disorderly
conduct and an additional $10 for carrying concealed weapons. In

January 1870, Jim Porter was sentenced to two years in the penitentiary for cow stealing. One month later the court dismissed charges against the notorious chicken thief "Pigfoot" with a caution to "vamose this ranche or dire calamities would befall him." Murder was also a grim reality. In December 1869, a railroad laborer struck a fellow worker on the head with a spade "in such a violent manner as to leave him bleeding and stunned." The worker died the next day from the effects of the assault.[10]

In 1870, Houston's business district was tightly clustered along Buffalo Bayou and Congress Street. The majority of Houston's thirty-seven lawyers lived around Courthouse Square, which was bordered by Congress, Preston, Fannin, and San Jacinto streets. The county courthouse, built in 1860, was a two-story brick structure that faced Congress. The Pillot Building on the corner of Congress and Fannin was "a busy hub of downtown business." Lawyers like W.P. Hamblen, E. P. Turner, and the firm of Cline & Usher had their offices in its two upper floors. By the 1890s, many lawyers had their offices in the five-story Binz Building—Houston's first "skyscraper."[11]

Colonel John H. Manley, the association's first vice-president, had his office at the corner of Fannin and Preston, on the southwest corner of the Courthouse Square. The historian B. H. Carroll wrote that the majority of Houston's brilliant lawyers "confined themselves to the practice of civil law but one or two won name and fame as criminal lawyers." Colonel John H. Manley was one such man. According to Carroll, Manley was "one of the greatest criminal lawyers who ever practiced at the Houston Bar."[12]

George Goldthwaite, the association's second vice-president, had his office a good two blocks from the courthouse in the Insurance Building at the corner of Main and Franklin. His success as counsel for the Texas Central Railroad earned him the reputation of being "one of the most invincible practitioners at the Texas bar" and "one of the best corporation lawyers in the country." During Houston's municipal fiscal crisis in 1868, Goldthwaite drafted an economic plan that curtailed the city's spiraling inflation and influenced Houston's "politics and economics for over twenty years."[13]

Located next to the Pillot Building and directly across from the courthouse on Fannin Street was Gray's Building. Judge James R.

Masterson's office was located on the second floor of Gray's Building, across the hall from the law office of Gray & Botts.

By the time Peter W. Gray was elected the first president of the association in 1870, his reputation as a distinguished jurist was well established. In February 1874, Governor Coke appointed Gray to the Supreme Court as an associate justice. But poor health led him to resign his position and he returned to Houston, where he died on October 3, 1874, after thirty-four years of legal service. Although Gray suffered from "bad health and nervous irritability" throughout his life and was "sometimes quick and testy in his manners," he was "like a father" to the young men of his profession.[14]

Little is known about the activities of these men within the first HBA due to the absence of internal records. Sometime during the early 1870s, however, the HBA dissolved its charter and did not formally re-emerge until its reorganization in 1901. But even though the HBA was dormant for a time, the leading members of the Houston bar remained active.

At the state level, Houston lawyers were involved in the organization of the Texas Bar Association in July 1882. Of its initial 307 members, thirteen were from Houston and included such men as James A. Baker, Sr., James A. Baker, Jr., W. B. Botts, W. H. Crank, W. P. Hamblen, and E. P. Turner—all members of the original Houston Bar Association. In 1884, W. H. Crank served on the Committee on Legal Education and Admission to the Bar, and during the 1880s and 1890s, lawyers from Baker & Botts consistently filled the positions on the Committee on Commercial Law.[15] Between the organization of the Texas Bar Association (in 1882) and 1910, four of Houston's most prominent lawyers served as president of the association: Norman G. Kittrell, 1890–1891; Presley K. Ewing, 1899–1900; Lewis R. Bryan, 1902–1903; and Hiram M. Garwood, 1905–1906.

Time and again, the names of Houston's prominent lawyers appear in the history of Houston's economic development. Some served as mayor, some as members of local, state, and federal government, and others as "city builders." Houston's leading lawyers realized that they had a civic responsibility to assist in the development of their city. It also made sense to do so from a financial standpoint. Lawyers were a segment of Houston's "aggressive business elite" who "correctly understood that their personal careers and fortunes were tied directly to the fate of the city's economy."[16]

One of these men was John Henry Kirby. When he arrived in Houston in 1890, he was a lawyer by training and an entrepreneur at heart. Once in Houston, he set up a law office in the Commercial National Bank. In addition to his legal practice, Kirby was involved in Houston real estate and in East Texas timber lands. Although he was yet to achieve fame as a legendary timber baron, he was known in business circles as a "go-getter."[17] The Cotton Exchange of Houston noted his enthusiasm and selected him to travel to Washington, D.C., to resolve the Morgan's Point right-of-way dispute, which was impeding ship traffic on Buffalo Bayou. By 1901, Kirby was senior partner of "the highly reputable firm of Kirby, Martin, and Eagle," but his primary interest was in developing a timber empire.[18] He achieved his goal in July 1901, with the incorporation of the Houston Oil–Kirby Lumber Company.

Houston lawyers figured prominently in the development of the Houston Ship Channel. Initially hailed as nothing but a dream and called the "damndest fake out of door" by Galvestonians, the channel was the product of a few visionaries who believed in the project and Houston's future. Leading the movement were two of Houston's eminent members of the bench and bar, Joseph C. Hutcheson and Thomas H. Ball. John Henry Kirby also played a major role in bringing deep water to Houston. In 1892, Kirby journeyed to Washington, D.C., to meet with Congressman Charles Stewart and resolve the issue of the "obstruction to Buffalo Bayou navigation at Morgan's Point."[19] The success of Kirby's mission allowed Houston to move ahead on the actual dredging of the channel. While Kirby cleared a major physical hurdle, it was Hutcheson and Ball, who, as Houston's U.S. Congressmen, secured the necessary federal funds.

Although Charles Stewart was a lawyer and early member of the HBA, it was not until Hutcheson succeeded Stewart to Congress in 1892 that a proposition was "even ever submitted to Congress involving a greater depth of water than the twelve foot canal which was then operated chiefly for the benefit of the Houston Direct Navigation Company." Through the efforts of Hutcheson in the House, as well as through his close friend Roger Q. Mills in the

Senate, the government appointed an "eminent Board of Engineers
. . . for the purpose of surveying and reporting upon the project."
Upon Hutcheson's retirement from the House of Representatives in
1896, Thomas H. Ball carried on the work of Hutcheson and
successfully passed a bill that created a deep-water ship channel for
Houston.[20] Despite Federal approval, the work proceeded at a slow
pace. By 1908, Mayor Horace Baldwin Rice was impatient with the
slow progress and wanted to press ahead and have the city complete
the project. Once again, it was Ball who provided an innovative
solution. He proposed the creation of a navigation district that would
have the "power to issue bonds for one-half the amount necessary to
complete the 25-foot project."[21] As Ball predicted, Congress did
"jump at the offer," and the deep-water project was completed in
1914. In his history of the Port of Houston, Ball wrote that "prior
to Houston's offer, no substantial contribution had ever been made
by local interests to secure the adoption of their projects."[22] With
the help of Judge W. H. Wilson and T. H. Stone, Ball later
engineered the creation of the Harris County Houston Ship Channel
Navigation District. When it came time to campaign for the original
$1.25 million bond issue that was needed to bring deep water to
Houston, two lawyers stood out as "ardent campaigners": Chester
H. Bryan and Colonel Jacob F. Wolters.[23] Ball served as counsel for
the Port of Houston from 1911 to 1931.

Before Ball left Washington, D.C., Frank Andrews paid him a visit
and offered Ball a position as his new law partner. Ball accepted the
offer "without hesitation," but he did confess to Andrews that his
involvement with the ship channel project might allow only minimal
time for law. Andrews was delighted with Ball's acceptance; as to
Ball's concern about minimal time for law, Andrews said:

> We'll both be permanently located in Houston, and expected to
> 'do our bit' in helping to build the city. I want you to do whatever
> you deem necessary, giving required time thereto, as a contribu-
> tion from the firm.[24]

In 1902, they organized the firm of Andrews and Ball. Over time,
other distinguished lawyers such as Judge Sam Streetman, John A.
Mobley, and John G. Logue were associated with the firm. After

Andrews's death, the HBA memorialized him by saying that no man "took a more active or aggressive interest in [Houston's] growth."[25]

Samuel H. Brashear was another prominent member of the Houston bar. As a judge he was "not afraid to venture out into new fields" because he was "a lawyer worthy of the steel of any foeman."[26] Always interested in politics, Brashear ran for mayor in 1898 and defeated incumbent H. Baldwin Rice on a platform of urban progressivism. Brashear believed that the "city government should be instrumental in uplifting both the physical and social conditions of city life."[27] During his administration Brashear expanded governmental responsibility for the welfare of the community and pursued policies that promoted social justice. Fashioning himself as the champion of the little man, Brashear staunchly resisted the Northern capitalists and their monopoly of utility corporations. To that end, his push for public ownership of all utilities and a municipal electric plant "met with mounting resistance by the utility companies as well as growing consternation among the commercial-civic elite."[28] After a protracted deadlock on the municipal ownership issue, Brashear resigned in January 1901 and returned to his law practice.

At the turn of the century the Houston Bar Association served an urban bar in a rapidly growing city. Historian B. H. Carroll wrote that Houston's early lawyers were "men of probity and honor, of skill and power, of learning and eloquence, of old fashioned courtesy and chivalrous consideration, of chaste diction and faultless bearing, who gave the Bar of Harris County its high standards, its legal ambitions and its lofty ethics."[29] But as Houston's population grew, so did the number of those who wished to practice law in the city. In 1900, Houston had 187 lawyers and a population of 44,633.[30] It is questionable, moreover, whether those lawyers new to Houston were all of decent character and ability, despite Carroll's glowing description.

In 1884, Oran M. Roberts of the Texas Bar Association warned that an individual's "good looks, sharpness and appearance" did not guarantee he possessed good legal qualifications.[31] Nevertheless, the admissions standard to the bar, or more precisely, the absence of a standard in the 1870s and '80s enabled a number of unqualified individuals to gain admittance to the ranks of the profession. An aspiring lawyer either read law books on his own, or he studied law under a practicing lawyer. Once he had acquired some degree of legal knowledge, he went to a county judge and obtained a certificate that affirmed his status as a Texas resident for a minimum of six months, that he was at least twenty-one years old, and that he was of sound moral character. The individual then presented his certificate to a Supreme Court justice or district judge for final approval and licensing. Often the judge would appoint a committee of lawyers to orally examine the applicant's legal expertise. The examination, however, was often nothing more than a drinking session.[32]

For example, when John Henry Kirby was admitted to the bar in 1885, he, like most other men who wished to practice law, prepared himself simply by reading law in a law office. His "bar examination" consisted of oral questioning by lawyers appointed by the district judge. One of the first questions put to Kirby during his examination was whether he had enough money on him to pay for the "examination bottle" needed to toast the candidate upon his successful completion of the exam. Like most lawyers of their day, Kirby's questioners took for granted that the examinee was sufficiently equipped to enter the legal profession.[33]

During the 1880s, the Texas Bar Association lobbied for a provision that automatically licensed applicants who had graduated from a reputable law school, and in 1891, the Texas legislature passed such an act.[34] When Houston built a new courthouse in 1883, leading lawyers organized two associations that focused on legal education. The Houston Law Students Library Association organized on September 28, 1896. John B. Ashe was president, Tracy B. Dunn, vice-president, Alfred R. Hamblen, secretary, and Louis A. Kottwitz, treasurer. Forty-eight members met every Tuesday night at the law office of William H. Crank and W. F. Carothers. Three years later, Alfred R. Hamblen became chairman of a new organization, the Houston Law Student Association. This organization started with fifteen members and met every Thursday night in Lewis A. Kottwitz's office in the Binz Building.[35]

Compounding the problem of lawyers of questionable ability was the increase in lawsuits in general due to the city's rapid expansion. A Houston souvenir pamphlet published in 1893 for the World's Columbian Exposition boasted that Houston had "long passed through that siege of profligacy, crime and immorality which, sooner or later, must come to every growing western town."[36] However, the problem was that Houston was still growing and was struggling to cope with its industrial growth and urbanization. It must be noted that while the problems facing Houston at the close of the century were common to those faced by other cities, the city's solutions to these problems were often unique.

As the city grew, so did the miles of railroad track that served its streetcars. The regulation of the street railway companies presented a challenge to both the bar and the city government. On March 18, 1889, the track-laying crews of the rival Boyd Brothers and the Houston City Street Railway Company engaged in a "battle of the streets" near the corner of Congress and San Jacinto. Both companies were vying to lay track between the railroad station and the downtown hotels. Because it was unclear who had the right to lay track and control the traffic on these thoroughfares, each company laid its "ties and rails with all the haste possible" and endeavored to "outwit and circumvent the other."[37] For the better part of the morning, the two crews raced "nip and tuck" to the delight of spectators who lined the street. The arrival of Sheriff Ellis with a court injunction against further construction brought the festivities to an end. On March 19, the *Houston Daily Post* reported that "prominent counsel has been engaged on both sides, and the fight promises to be a lively one."[38]

That afternoon "a large and interested crowd of spectators thronged the district court" to hear the respective counsels, City Attorney Henry F. Ring for the city, and Mr. Garnett for the Houston City Street Railway Company (HCSRC). Garnett argued that the injunction should be dismissed because the HCSRC was a legitimate state-licensed franchise, and that it had always operated under its charter from the state. Boyd Brothers, on the other hand, did not possess the required license that allowed the city to hire it in the first place. Garnett charged that allowing Boyd "full opportunity to build his line" while tying the hands of the HCSRC was "a bare-faced, unblushing fraud on the part of the mayor and city officers" to deprive the HCSRC of its rights. Garnett was careful to exclude City Attorney Henry F. Ring from the list of fraudulent city officials.[39]

Ring countered that the issue was "whether or not the Houston Street Railway Company had the right, whenever it pleased, to go upon any thoroughfare it saw fit and, without obtaining the consent of the council, lay its tracks wherever it wanted to." The city ordinances stated that it did not. Three days later Judge Masterson ruled that Boyd Brothers could no longer lay track over the thoroughfares used by the HCSRC, that the HCSRC had to remove the new track it laid on Congress during the "battle of the streets," and that no company could build a railroad in Houston without first obtaining a permit from the city council.[40]

The courthouse was not the only place in town for entertainment. Houston's spirited social life centered around saloons with such colorful names as "The Shades," "Solo," "Revolving Light," "The Sample Room," and the "Iron Clad," a gambling house named for the sheet iron that covered its second story. Technically, gambling houses were illegal, but the proprietors of such places had a special arrangement whereby they "pleaded guilty and paid a fixed fine" whenever they were indicted by the grand jury. According to Dr. S. O. Young, the grand jury would occasionally "get too inquisitive and get after a bunch of the players and then there was sure enough trouble." Such was the case when the grand jury indicted "a number of very prominent lawyers, doctors and business men" for "indulging in poker in a public place." To exonerate themselves, these prominent men hired Colonel Manley, who successfully defended them on the novel ground that "there was a bed in the room and that a bedroom was not a public place in the meaning of the law."[41]

Another more sensational criminal trial held the attention of Houstonians as the new century began—this one taking place not in Houston but in New York City. In 1900, as the first year of the new century came to a close, Houstonians followed the fate of attorney Albert T. Patrick, a Texas native on trial for his life for his part in the murder of wealthy philanthropist William Marsh Rice.[42]

Although Rice was not a man of letters, he admired East Coast colleges, and it was his dream to bequeath his vast fortune to the creation of a new, similar institution of higher learning in Houston. To oversee the building of this new institute, Rice named his closest friends as its trustees, including his friend and attorney Captain James A. Baker. Baker would later be called on to fight for the Institute and enforce his friend's bequest, as the elderly Rice's second wife, Julia Elizabeth Baldwin Rice, did not share her husband's dream. Mrs. Rice saw the donation of the entire Rice fortune to the creation of a college as a threat to what she felt was rightfully hers. Upon being informed by her attorney-cousin that divorcing Rice was not an option—at that time adultery was the only grounds for divorce in New York, where the couple had resided since their marriage—and being determined to claim what she felt was her rightful share of her husband's estate, Mrs. Rice sought a second opinion.

She consulted future Houston mayor and Harris County bar president Oran T. Holt, who had a reputation as a "society lawyer."[43] Holt advised Mrs. Rice that to take any action in New York would be futile because under the laws of that state Mrs. Rice was not entitled by right to claim any of her husband's property. Holt's strategy was for Mrs. Rice to persuade her husband to return to Texas and thereafter to stay married just long enough so that an eventual divorce could be governed by Texas' more favorable community property laws. Fortunately for the Rice Institute, Mrs. Rice did not see her plan come to fruition, though her attempt to claim for herself a part of the Rice fortune did trigger a protracted legal battle and led, if indirectly, to her husband's murder.

Mrs. Rice did not convince her husband to return to Houston, but she returned there herself, telling everyone that Houston was the couple's permanent home. Soon afterward, however, she became seriously ill, and perhaps sensing that her own death was imminent, she directed Oran Holt to draw up a new will for her. In this new will Mrs. Rice claimed Houston as her domicile and "gave away half of what she thought to be their communal property."[44] She died only a few months later.

When the county court of Harris County admitted Mrs. Rice's will to probate, William Marsh Rice filed suit in both Texas and New York against Oran Holt as executor of the will, challenging the validity of the will and the jurisdiction of the Texas court. To represent him in New York, Holt hired Albert T. Patrick, who had only recently moved to New York from Texas, where disbarment proceedings had been brought against him.[45]

Patrick saw his association with the Rice case as an opportunity to make himself a wealthy man. He convinced Rice's manservant, Charlie Jones, that it was unfair for the old man to leave his entire fortune to some non-existent school in Texas and to leave his most loyal employee without a penny. Jones, it appears, had a rather malleable character and was easily drawn into Patrick's plot to steal the Rice estate. Patrick forged a new will, this one naming him as executor and heir to the bulk of the Rice estate. Ironically, the manservant Jones was left out of even the forged will.

All that stood between Patrick and the Rice fortune was Rice himself. Though a man of more than eighty years, he was in remarkably good health. Patrick and Jones sought to hasten Rice's death by drugging his food with small doses of mercury, but Rice seemed to be unaffected. Finally, Patrick resolved that their approach should be more direct, and he orchestrated Rice's murder. With chloroform procured by Patrick and under Patrick's explicit instructions on how to use it, Jones carried out the murder. Patrick then called in a physician friend to pronounce Rice dead of natural causes.

Their plot began to unravel the next day, however, when another associate of Patrick's attempted to cash a forged check on Rice's account at S. M. Swenson & Sons. Suspicious, a Swenson's partner telephoned Rice's apartment only to be told by Jones that Rice had died the night before. S. M. Swenson & Sons then wired Captain Baker in Houston that they were suspicious as to the cause of Rice's death. Baker and Rice's brother, Frederick, left immediately for New York. "At each train stop," writes historian Marie P. McAshan, "newspapers were announcing Albert T. Patrick the wealthy Rice's sole heir."[46]

Captain Baker was concerned about the "Patrick will" because it left a mere $250,000 to the Rice Institute.[47] Upon arriving in New York, Baker and Frederick Rice enlisted the cooperation of the district attorney's office and launched an investigation into Rice's sudden death and the suspect will. Within two weeks Patrick and Jones were indicted for forgery of the will and other documents. When Rice's autopsy revealed traces of mercury, Jones confessed that he and Patrick had murdered Rice. Although Jones's confession discredited the Patrick will and solved the mystery of who killed Rice, the disposition of the Elizabeth Rice will remained unresolved.

Returning to Houston, Baker faced Oran Holt and a host of distant Rice relatives and Houston charitable organizations that were named as beneficiaries in the Rices' wills. Realizing that a protracted legal battle would endanger the Rice Institute, Baker moved to settle out of court. Although it took more than $1 million to pay lawyers' fees, executors' commissions, and Rice's own bequests to relatives and charities, Baker's deft negotiating preserved a beginning endowment of more than $4.6 million.[48]

Along with the founding of the Rice Institute, the new century brought economic growth to Houston. The Galveston hurricane in September 1900 effectively ended the fifty-year Houston-Galveston city rivalry for economic superiority. The Spindletop gusher in January 1901 guaranteed that Houston would be the focal point of something big in the foreseeable future, and Houston's push for a deep-water channel was well under way, thanks to boosters like Judge Hutcheson and Thomas H. Ball. But despite this growth, all was not well in the Magnolia City. The boom brought thousands to Houston each month looking to strike it rich. The Spindletop strike made Houston the center of the new "black gold" rush, but that distinction also brought crime and vice. The rapid influx of "wildcatters" and others seeking opportunity in the boom stretched the limits of the civil and criminal justice system. Lawlessness returned to Houston, and the city assumed a frontier atmosphere as "pistol toting" and street gunfights became regular occurrences. The violence reached a crescendo in the summer and fall of 1901, when five men, three of whom were police officers, died in two separate gunfights.

A *Houston Chronicle* editorial for October 10, 1901, claimed that nine out of ten murders in Texas were "traceable to the all too promiscuous habit that men have in Texas of going about the country with bloody six-shooters concealed upon their persons." The newspaper pledged to use whatever influence it might have "to arouse . . . opposition to the pernicious practice" of carrying deadly weapons. The *Chronicle* was particularly concerned about a recent tragedy whereby a policeman failed to arrest four known pistol "toters" that were inside an illegally open saloon. It strongly criticized those public officials for "laxity in performance of official duty" and predicted that unless the community did something to force a change, a day would come when "some 'pistol toter' will open up a fusillade on the streets of Houston and kill some innocent bystander."[49] In the same edition, a letter appeared from Judge E. P. Hamblen addressed to the editor. Hamblen praised the efforts of the *Chronicle* in raising public sentiment "to bring about the enforcement of our laws," but he criticized the police force for doing "very little to enforce the law" when they were "fully aware" that laws were "violated daily in a flagrant manner."

In 1901, two major shootings occurred on the street in front of Yadon's saloon at the corner of Congress and San Jacinto. The first shooting occurred during the early morning hours of July 30, 1901, when John Vaughn shot police officer William Weiss through the heart. The tragedy was further heightened by the fact that the previous day Vaughn had been arrested and taken to the police station for "discharging a pistol through a window in his apartment."[50] Vaughn had been jailed for only eight hours and released that night.

Upon leaving the police station, Vaughn immediately visited his lawyer, Henry E. Kahn, of the law firm Brockman & Kahn. Vaughn claimed that he had lost his watch and $25 while under arrest and that he needed assistance in dealing with the arresting officer, Herman Youngst. Kahn agreed to help Vaughn, and the two men set out for the police station. On the way, they ran into officers Weiss and Youngst in front of Yadon's saloon. Youngst told Kahn that he knew nothing about Vaughn's watch or money but that it "was probably at the police station." Kahn then advised his client that they would have to wait until morning to get his belongings.[51]

While Kahn was inside the saloon enjoying a drink with an old friend, Vaughn and his brother got into an argument with officer Weiss. Motioning to Weiss, Vaughn suggested to his brother that "maybe he got it." According to a witness, Weiss then raised his club and said, "Don't you accuse me of anything like that." When Weiss stepped toward Vaughn, Vaughn drew a pistol and shot Weiss four times at close range. Vaughn immediately fled the scene but, after a running gun battle down Franklin and Fannin streets, was mortally wounded by police and soon died.[52]

Houston's two newspapers continued to wage a vigorous campaign against the growing crime and corruption throughout the fall of 1901. With a shooting every month, it was not difficult for the press to buttress its attacks with glaring examples of crime. The *Chronicle* was especially vehement in denouncing police officers who "turn a deaf ear and blind eye to violations of law." A growing controversy over Police Chief John G. Blackburn's professionalism only added to the problem. Blackburn claimed that he did not have a "free hand" to create the type of police force he wanted and that it was impossible for the police department to get the criminal activity under control because the police lacked support. Specifically, he criticized the court and lawyers for impeding justice and tolerating "shysters," which Judge Norman G. Kittrell defined as "men willing to get results by any kind of method, however devious."[53]

In late October 1901, a group of Houstonians "high in social and business circles" hoped to aid police by organizing "a non-secret, non-religious and non-political organization for the prevention of high crime." Despite an increase in the number of arrests of pistol toters after the organization's creation, one prominent Houstonian complained that the accused were usually acquitted because defense attorneys insisted on a jury trial and effectively argued that the habit of carrying weapons was "almost universal." Constable W. W. Glass too felt that the police officers and courts were "not altogether to blame for the lax enforcement of laws." The constable believed that attorneys were at fault for continuing cases "until the witnesses are worn out" and seeking appeals when a rare conviction was obtained in the lower courts.[54]

The Houston City Council, however, placed the blame on the police department's poor performance, and it launched an investigation into the charges of police corruption. Because of the poor relations between the police department and the city council, Chief Blackburn offered to tender his resignation as chief of police and leave it to "the citizens of Houston to decide this question." Blackburn's only stipulation was that the alderman who had been antagonistic to him also had to resign. The resignations did not happen, and the dispute continued.[55]

Faced with a *de facto* vote of "no confidence" from the city council and persistent criticism from the local press, Chief Blackburn struck back and blamed the "shyster" lawyer for Houston's law-enforcement problems. Claiming to have "specific charges and facts" against several Houston lawyers, Blackburn offered to assist "any member of the bar association . . . who felt like clarifying the moral atmosphere by kicking out the unworthy brothers." The "bar association" did not immediately react to Blackburn's offer.[56]

The December term of the criminal district court opened on Monday, December 2, 1901. Because of the increase in crime and the controversy surrounding Blackburn and the police department,

Judge Augustus C. Allen delivered an "unusually elaborate charge to the grand jury, touching upon all the usual violations of the law, among which he specifically mentioned pistol carrying and operating or playing of slot machines or other gambling devices."[57]

As the new session of the district court got under way, James B. Brockman was defending a client in LaGrange. Brockman was "one of the most distinguished criminal lawyers in the country" and "a Christian citizen and a real man, in the highest sense of the word." He always fought hard for his client, even if it led to his own incarceration. During the trial in LaGrange, Brockman interrupted the proceedings and accused the prosecution of misquoting testimony during closing arguments. The presiding judge warned Brockman to quiet down, but Brockman persisted in his objection. Finally, the judge found Brockman in contempt of court and ordered him jailed for 24 hours. Brockman used his entitled phone call to contact his partner, Henry E. Kahn, back in Houston, who immediately set out for LaGrange to bail his friend out of jail. One week later Brockman faced a more serious problem when Houston's second major gunfight of 1901 erupted in front of Yadon's saloon.[58]

On December 11, 1901, at about 4 p.m., Sid Preacher and his friend W. C. Woodward were standing in front of the saloon when they were approached by detective John C. James, who wanted to take Woodward in "on suspicion." When Woodward asked to see a warrant, James replied that he did not need one. When Preacher protested that Woodward was not going anywhere without a warrant, James allegedly grabbed Woodward by the shirt collar and started to haul him off. At that point, Preacher "ran to the buggy and came back with his shotgun." When James "jerked out his pistol," Preacher shot him. As Detective James "fell to his knees and rolled into the gutter," Officer Herman Youngst rushed to the scene and tried to wrench the shotgun from Preacher's hands. Failing to do so, Youngst turned to escape but Preacher shot him in the back. When Youngst did not go down, Preacher "ran in on him and struck him three or four times over the head with the shotgun." In his final moments, James raised his pistol from the gutter and fired a fatal shot at Preacher. The tragedy of the three deaths was further heightened by the arrest of James B. Brockman later that night for allegedly having instructed his client, Preacher, to shoot the next officer who tried to arrest him without a warrant.[59]

Sid Preacher was a young man with a reputation for trouble. After stabbing his stepfather, Preacher went on to spend the rest of his life in and out of courts. On the day before the fatal shooting he had been under arrest for "running a gaming device" in a saloon. On the way to the police station, the arresting officers allowed Preacher to visit Brockman. When Preacher asked him whether he could be punished for killing a police officer who tried to arrest him without a warrant, Brockman told Preacher that "the law would probably acquit him, as the court of criminal appeals had decided that a man had that right." Despite Brockman's warning to Preacher that he would end up like John Vaughn if he did shoot an officer, the impressionable Preacher had heard what he wanted to hear—and so had the two officers accompanying him. According to their later testimony, Brockman told Preacher to cooperate with the police and "go with this man this time." Brockman, however, added that it was "getting to be a pretty come-off that men are getting arrested every day and thrown in jail down there without a warrant." He then allegedly told Preacher: "You arm yourself with a six shooter, and the next policeman who attempts to arrest you without a warrant for any offense, except for carrying a six shooter, shoot his belly off."[60]

The next morning, Deputy Chief Thompson made a special request of the *Chronicle:* "I want you to state that a Houston lawyer is the cause of all the trouble and that I, myself, made the complaint. I've lived here since '46 and know what I am speaking of." Chief Blackburn seized the moment to criticize lawyers, claiming that there was little he could do "when men strike against me by advising their clients to kill my men when they are doing their duty." Blackburn claimed that despite having arrested "suspicious characters and bunco steerers and concealed weapon carriers by the hundred," he was powerless because the courts refused to stand by him. He also added that Brockman would not "run this department in the future."[61]

After the shooting, friends of Brockman warned him that the police were out to lynch him and that he should stay out of public places. Although not convinced that someone was out to get him, Brockman purchased two shotguns for his office. Later that night, the police arrested Brockman and charged him with murder. Though not a friend of Brockman, Attorney John Lovejoy offered his services without fee because he believed that the "misguided action of the officers" and the arrest of Brockman was "a great and dangerous wrong to the entire citizenship of Houston." When Brockman appeared before Judge Augustus C. Allen, he demanded a public hearing to exonerate his name and argued that "the men who procured my imprisonment knew the charge was as false as hell!'"[62]

On December 12, the lawyers of Houston met in Judge Wilson's courtroom to elect a special judge to preside over the court during Judge Wilson's illness. After the lawyers selected Judge W. P. Hamblen as special judge, J. M. Coleman asked them to remain in order to "discuss a matter that was of vital importance." Citing Chief Blackburn's recent charges that shyster lawyers were impeding the administration of justice and that he had evidence against such practitioners, Coleman claimed that the "unfortunate tragedy of yesterday renders it of extreme importance that we act now and here." Those assembled in the room agreed, but Mr. Lovejoy cautioned that any bar committee or association should not "enter into any political questions" because that was "outside the sphere of the members of this bar." The chairman, Oran T. Holt, appointed a committee on the permanent organization of the bar association consisting of Presley K. Ewing, Hiram Garwood, W. H. Crank, E. P. Hamblen, and Mr. Gibson. He also appointed Lovejoy, J. K. P. Gillespie, and J. M. Coleman to a committee to meet with Chief Blackburn and review his allegations and evidence.[63]

On December 14, 1901, "fully 100 lawyers" met in the Eleventh District Court and formally organized the Harris County Bar Association. The primary reason for organizing a bar association was to refute Chief Blackburn's charges of lawyer corruption and to weed out the corrupt few that were giving the profession a bad name. Although R. J. Thacker refused to enroll his name as a member of the association and "was greatly in evidence and insisted on being heard on every question," most of those present were in favor of organizing an association, and fifty-three lawyers enrolled as charter members. The objects of the association were to "advance, promote and uphold the wonted honor, dignity and ethical standard of the profession . . . and to encourage cordial social intercourse among its members." Membership was open to any Harris County attorney in "honorable standing." The initiation fee and the annual dues were each $2.50.[64]

The members of the Harris County Bar Association elected Oran T. Holt, president; Presley K. Ewing, vice-president; John B. Ashe, secretary; and J. I. Wilson, treasurer. President Holt created four initial committees: the Executive Committee; the Committee on Admission of Members, chaired by W. H. Crank; the Committee on Grievances and Discipline; and the Committee on Investigation, chaired by J. M. Coleman. Prior to Christmas, the Committee on Investigation found damaging evidence against some ten lawyers, but the grand jury exonerated Brockman. After a thorough investigation, District Attorney Lea reported that he had "found no evidence whatever on which to found a prosecution." The case against Brockman was dismissed.[65]

Like the 1870 Houston Bar Association before it, the Harris County Bar Association was relatively short-lived. Having accomplished its initial purpose with the exoneration of one of its eminent brethren, the Harris County Bar Association soon disbanded. In both cases, once the challenges that galvanized Houston's lawyers and spurred them to action had been met, the associations they formed to meet those challenges became inactive and were dissolved. Not until Houston lawyers concerned themselves with the ongoing work of shaping the direction of the legal profession was a permanent bar association to become a reality in Houston.

After serving his term as bar president, Oran T. Holt ran for mayor in 1902, with the endorsement of the Houston Business League. As president of the Harris County Bar Association, Holt led the bar in its crusade to purge itself of unworthy members who tarnished the profession. As mayor, Holt left his mark by promoting a "spirit of compromise" between the municipal government and Northern franchise owners.[66] In contrast to Samuel H. Brashear's administration, which fostered a policy of confrontation in government-business relations, Holt encouraged the city council to pursue vigorously a "course of accommodation with the Northern-owned utility corporations." This reconciliation was critical "in securing a steady flow of Northern capital to underwrite Houston's oil industry, shipping facilities, and other public works projects." Holt's policy of accommodation reflected the emergence across the country of the scientific manager "as the preferred director of public policy." In Houston, corporate lawyers typically "took over the negotiations between the city council and franchise holders."[67]

On the evening of March 26, 1904, forty-seven Houston lawyers met in the office of Hamblen, Scott & Hamblen to discuss the organizing of a permanent bar association and the arrangements for entertaining visiting lawyers at the upcoming meeting of the Texas Bar Association. The question of arranging entertainment was soon superseded by the more important task of organizing a permanent local bar association. During the meeting, Thomas H. Ball stated: "We should have an organization so that we could discuss at all times matters of interest and aid in maintaining the high standards of ethics in our profession, and bring about social relations among the members of our profession." John Charles Harris echoed the sentiments of "cultivating a social spirit" by proclaiming that he was in favor of organizing a bar association "if we don't do anything but give an annual dinner." Ira P. Jones was enthusiastic about a bar association because it would bring lawyers closer together: "I would much rather practice with men with whom I am acquainted than with those whom I don't know, and then when I lose a case it doesn't worry me as much." Another lawyer added: "Houston's bar already has great influence over the State and will be extended by forming an organization. This is the day of unions, and why shouldn't we have one?"[68]

The other lawyers greeted the proposal with enthusiasm and adopted a constitution that had been drafted a week earlier by the committee of Frank Andrews, W. H. Wilson, Jonathan Lane, F. S. Burke, Lewis Bryan, Ben Campbell, and G. W. Tharp. The constitution formally named the organization the Houston Bar Association and declared that the objectives of the organization were "to promote the good standing of the legal profession, and preserve its ethics, and to promote social relations between its members." Before the meeting adjourned, Judge E. P. Hamblen was elected unanimously as president, J. I. Wilson as secretary, and Judge G. W. Tharp as treasurer.[69]

The 1904 HBA constitution called for regular meetings of the association "not less than every three months" and "at least one annual social reunion." The affairs of the HBA were "managed and conducted by a board of directors consisting of twelve members appointed by the president.'' The directors were appointed for a term of three years. With the power to appoint all directors, the president possessed considerable authority. Beginning in 1904, the members of the association held an annual meeting on the last Saturday in December for the exclusive purpose of electing a president, a secretary, and a treasurer.[70]

Membership in the HBA was open to all members of the ''Harris County Bar, in good standing, both socially and professionally.'' However, at least on paper, the procedure for becoming a member tightly controlled who actually joined the association. Those wishing to join had to submit an application to the president that was ''endorsed and vouched for by three members of the association in good standing.'' The application then went before the association, where four-fifths of the members present had to vote in favor by secret ballot. Once admitted, the admission fee was $5 and the annual dues were $3.[71]

Unlike Houston's two earlier bar associations, the 1904 HBA became a viable institution. Although Houston lawyers were still concerned about ''shysters'' and ''ambulance chasers,'' the HBA succeeded because it placed an even greater emphasis on cultivating ''social relations between its members.'' Beginning in 1905, the HBA held an annual dinner banquet at some of Houston's finest restaurants. A Shakespearian quote appearing in the dinner program of the fourth annual banquet exemplified the social nature of the HBA: ''Do as adversaries at the law; strive mightily, but eat and drink like friends.''[72]

The HBA's accomplishments in 1905 removed any doubts about the permanency of the association. Under the leadership of Major F. Charles Hume, Sr., the HBA stepped into judicial politics and adopted a resolution that supported an increase in the salaries of state judges.[73] The HBA also campaigned successfully for a new county courthouse. Of the present ''antiquated ruin,'' one prominent Houstonian complained that the courthouse had ''long outgrown its days of use'' and that Harris County had for its capitol building ''a structure that might disgrace a country precinct.'' In March 1905, the HBA took action and petitioned the county commissioners to institute steps for the construction of a new courthouse. Taking notice of the HBA's active interest in the project, the *Houston Daily Post* commended the association for its "forward move toward securing a new courthouse."[74]

Designed by the Dallas architectural firm of Lang & Witchell, the courthouse featured classical revival styling and a large domed roof. The interior included such amenities as two elevators, an ice-water drinking system, and, for the first time in Texas, a jury bedroom complete with cots and linen.[75] County Judge A. E. Amerman and the members of the commissioners court took great pride in the fact that such a "superb building" was constructed without any hint of scandal. Houstonians were not only proud of their new courthouse, but optimistic as well. Said one contemporary: "The stupendous [legal] transactions in men's lives may perhaps be given a shade more of the dignity that belongs to them because they are enacted in a theatre better appointed and more commodious and comfortable."[76]

The formal dedication of the new courthouse on March 2, 1911, marked the beginning of a new period in the history of the HBA. Before 1911, the HBA's early history was characterized by sporadic meetings and members who met "on call" to resolve some crisis. Although meetings of Houston's first two bar associations did attract high attendance and elicit a high level of enthusiasm, any long-range plans for action and reform were short-lived. But by 1911, with a membership of ninety-nine lawyers and an annual operating budget of $326.80, the Houston Bar Association was well on its way to ensuring a lasting role for itself in Houston's unfolding history.[77]

CHAPTER THREE

Adjusting to Change, 1911–1940

From its inception in 1870, the HBA sought to advance the science of jurisprudence by establishing a law library. In 1910, President John Charles Harris calculated that subscriptions totaling $5,000 were needed to finalize the creation of an association library. After a dismal response, Harris told the HBA: "I regret to say that we were not successful in establishing the foundation for an Association Library, as out of a total membership of one hundred and one, but nineteen members returned their written subscriptions to me." Although disappointed, Harris did not give up. To obtain the necessary funds for a library, he suggested that the HBA incorporate without capital stock and support the creation of a "Literary Association."[1]

Three years later, under President Wilmer S. Hunt, the HBA implemented John C. Harris's plan for funding a law library, and in March 1913 the Harris County Law Library was created under the charter of "Lawyers' Library Association." Judge Charles E. Ashe was the association's first president, Lewis R. Bryan the vice-president, Captain James A. Baker the treasurer, and R. W. Franklin the secretary. Housed in the Civil Courts Building, the library officially opened on October 1, 1915, and was available to all judges and lawyers practicing in or visiting Harris County. The Lawyers' Library Association paid Mr. F. W. Nisbet the "munificent salary of

$50 per month" to serve as the librarian, secretary, and treasurer. Judge James Autry contributed significantly to the success of the new library by donating $15,000 to the association. His only request was that the library should "always be open to the free use of struggling young lawyers."[2]

With the establishment of the new library, the HBA had successfully accomplished one of its original goals. The other goal, that of "raising the standard of the legal profession," would prove more elusive. Debate over the role of the lawyer in a changing society and defining the limits of that role would continue throughout the first decades of the twentieth century, and indeed up to the present day.

During the early 1900s, advocates of social activism throughout the United States began to challenge the purpose of bar associations and to attack what was seen as an elitist philosophy. Such criticism sparked debate within the legal profession over the proper role of the bar in an increasingly industrialized and urbanized society. The result was an acknowledgment that bar associations should strive to be more than social clubs and that the profession needed to more forcefully exert itself in providing services to the community. Exactly what these "services" should be, however, remained a hotly contested issue throughout the early decades of the twentieth century.[3]

The HBA's expansion in both membership and services to the Houston community from 1911 to 1941 was typical of the national trend in the legal profession to be more active in local communities. As an organization, the HBA began to grapple with the legal issues of the day and the role of the voluntary bar in society. But the discussion of issues did not always translate into positive action. Sporadic and often less-than-spectacular results demonstrated that any tangible accomplishment was due to the individual leadership and initiative of a given president and board of directors. During these formative years of the HBA, the evolutionary growth in the association's scope and function depended on the leadership and goals of individual presidents.

A problem for any HBA president was the constant struggle to balance the needs of his practice with those of the association. A typical law office had "but few law clerks, one or two stenographers, and perhaps an engrosser." The partners themselves often wrote the

(continued on page 59)

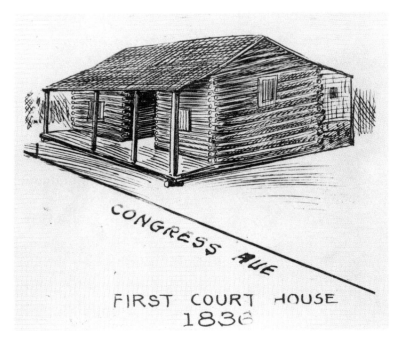

A sketch of Houston's first courthouse.

The 300 block of Main Street as it appeared in 1866. Courtesy Houston Metropolitan Research Center, Houston Public Library.

Houston lawyers met here in the newly remodeled Harris County Courthouse on April 23, 1870, to form the first Houston Bar Association.

*Peter W. Gray,
the "Father of the Bar."*

The Pillot Building was a "busy hub of downtown business." Above: A sketch from 1869. Below: As it appears today. Sketch courtesy Houston Metropolitan Research Center, Houston Public Library.

The five-story Binz Building was Houston's first skyscraper. Courtesy Houston Metropolitan Research Center, Houston Public Library.

Thomas H. Ball was the driving force behind the building of the Houston Ship Channel.

John Henry Kirby, one of Houston's "city builders." Courtesy Houston Metropolitan Research Center, Houston Public Library.

Joseph C. Hutcheson. Courtesy Houston Metropolitan Research Center, Houston Public Library.

Trolley cars were an important means of transportation during the "Battle of the Streets" in 1889. Courtesy Houston Metropolitan Research Center, Houston Public Library.

Henry E. Kahn was the law partner of James B. Brockman. Courtesy Houston Metropolitan Research Center, Houston Public Library.

In 1901, lawyers met in the Harris County Courthouse to organize the Harris County Bar Association. Courtesy Houston Metropolitan Research Center, Houston Public Library.

Oran T. Holt: Society lawyer, Houston mayor, and president of the 1901 Harris County Bar Association. Courtesy Houston Metropolitan Research Center, Houston Public Library.

41

Judge E. P. Hamblen, 1904 HBA President. Courtesy Houston Metropolitan Research Center, Houston Public Library.

John Charles Harris, HBA President 1910–11. Courtesy Houston Metropolitan Research Center, Houston Public Library.

The HBA was the driving force behind the construction of the Harris County Courthouse, built in 1911. In 1939, the association remodeled a room on the fourth floor and opened its first administrative office.

The Houston Main Street docks and skyline, circa 1911. The dome of the new county courthouse is clearly visible at center left. Courtesy Houston Metropolitan Research Center, Houston Public Library.

Lewis R. Bryan was a distinguished lawyer who served as president of the Texas Bar Association in 1902–03 and as president of the HBA in 1911. In 1913, he helped organize the Harris County Law Library. Courtesy Houston Metropolitan Research Center, Houston Public Library.

The Houston central business district circa 1915. Courtesy Houston Metropolitan Research Center, Houston Public Library.

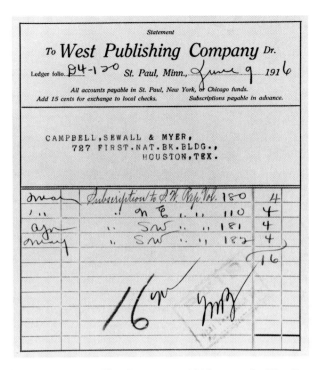

The administrative side of legal practice: a 1916 invoice for West Reporters.

Ben S. Campbell served two terms as Houston's mayor, from 1913–17. He demonstrated that the lawyer's new role as a "skilled negotiator and facilitator" was compatible with politics. Courtesy Houston Metropolitan Research Center, Houston Public Library.

Army life at Camp Logan. It was here that the Houston Riot of 1917 began. Courtesy Houston Metropolitan Research Center, Houston Public Library.

Jacob F. Wolters was one bar member who advocated swift punishment for those soldiers involved in the Houston Riot. Courtesy Houston Metropolitan Research Center, Houston Public Library.

Although World War I interrupted his legal career, Calvin B. Garwood later became a prominent lawyer, businessman, and civic leader. In 1935, he served as president of the HBA. Courtesy Houston Metropolitan Research Center, Houston Public Library.

William A. Vinson (pictured) formed a new law partnership in 1917 with Judge James A. Elkins.

47

These men opposed the Ku Klux Klan in the early 1920s. Right: As HBA President, J. W. Lockett raised the ethical standards of the bar. Below: Houston attorney Russell F. Wolters campaigned throughout Texas against Klan-endorsed candidates. Courtesy Houston Metropolitan Research Center, Houston Public Library.

HOUSTON BAR ASSOCIATION

December 26, 1929.

An example of an early HBA letterhead.

Captain James A. Baker: Savior of the Rice Institute, a key business leader during the Depression, and president of the HBA in 1931.

49

The "Suite 8F Crowd" held court in the Lamar Hotel. Courtesy Houston Metropolitan Research Center, Houston Public Library.

These two men fought constantly for the educational and legal legitimacy of their law school. Left: Jesse E. Moseley, President, Houston Law School. Right: Ewing Werlein, Dean, Houston Law School. Courtesy Houston Metropolitan Research Center, Houston Public Library.

The Houston Law School Class of 1934. Because the Houston Law School did not have its own building, classes were held in Harris County courtrooms.

David A. Simmons. His work as president of the Texas Bar Association had a great impact on the development of the HBA in the late 1930s. Courtesy State Bar of Texas.

J.S. Bracewell, founding father of the modern HBA. Photo courtesy Searcy Bracewell.

Houston Bar Association will have an old-fashioned bar banquet (as near as permissible) at Houston Club, Monday Night, February 5, at 7:00 o'clock. Stag. Informal. $1.50 per person. The new administration wants to pump some life into this association and this will be the starter. You will be furnished with real entertainment. We have two very good speakers for the occasion. No tiresome talks permitted. Entertainment Committee will call with tickets. Leave the aforesaid $1.50 with your stenographer in case you are out when a member of the committee calls. 100% attendance is expected.

                                        W. P. Hamblen,
                                            President.

An example of the type of invitation that infuriated women attorneys like Billye N. Russell.

Billye N. Russell.

Joyce Burg organized an informal group for women lawyers in 1933.

Lieutenant Colonel Leon Jaworski prosecuted Nazi war criminals at the close of World War II. Photo courtesy Mrs. Leon Jaworski.

After serving as HBA President in 1945, James L. Shepherd, Jr., served as president of the State Bar of Texas in 1946 and was later appointed chair of the American Bar Association House of Delegates in 1957.

George A. Butler expanded his firm in the postwar period.

The two men behind Houston's first Legal Aid Clinic: Judge Joseph C. Hutcheson, Jr., left, and Hugh Roy Cullen, right. Hutcheson provided the plan and Cullen provided the funds. Courtesy Houston *Magazine, Houston Chamber of Commerce.*

In 1952, Wilminor Carl became the first woman to serve on the HBA Board of Directors. Here President T. Everton Kennerly congratulates her on her victory.

In April 1960, HBA members and spouses enjoyed a seven-day "C.L.E. Cruise" to Jamaica.

HBA beach-party fun, circa 1960.

HBA President Harry Jones, left, Joyce Cox, Ruth Laws, Nelson Jones, and Richard Powell pose at an association function in 1952. Ruth Laws served as the HBA's executive secretary from 1939–1962.

In 1963, the HBA moved its office from the Harris County Courthouse to its second home, The Houston Club Building.

A gathering of judges and attorneys at The Houston Club.

A common sight at the Music Hall on Law Day.

Former HBA President Ewing Werlein and Mrs. Werlein, and Judge Allen Hannay, at the annual Federal Bar Association's reception for the judiciary.

As a young assistant district attorney in the early 1960s, Judge Carl Walker, Jr., petitioned the HBA for a desegregated association.

(continued from page 34)

arguments and briefs out in longhand.[4] The demands of a traditional two-partner practice left little time to devote to HBA issues, and by 1911 changes in the size and function of a law firm itself placed even greater demands on the president's time. The rise of corporations increased the need for specialization. As law firms grew in size to meet the legal needs of corporations, the "role of the lawyer evolved from advocate to counsel, and lawyers began to specialize, doing so out of the necessity of being competitive in a legal culture that was demanding increasing knowledge of practitioners."[5]

Although the expanding corporate practice was financially rewarding, the resulting atmosphere of competitiveness and the implementation of shrewd business tactics changed the public's perception of the legal profession. The image of the lawyer as "a skilled negotiator and facilitator, the practical man of business" supplanted the more lofty "nineteenth-century image of the law as a learned profession, with all that it implied in personal deference and respect, social prestige, and cultural power."[6] However much a necessary result of changing times, that new image ranked lawyers among other businessmen merely as players in the economic race to get ahead. With the rise of corporate practice, the public increasingly began to associate corporate lawyers, the advocates of big business, with the greed of big business. And in the process the legal profession surrendered a part of its traditional image as the vanguard of honesty and justice.

Paradoxically, the lawyer's new role as a "skilled negotiator and facilitator" uniquely qualified him for public office at a time when cities across the country were moving toward a more scientific and professional style of government. In Houston's 1913 mayoral election, a prominent lawyer again entered the political spotlight when incumbent H. Baldwin Rice announced that he would not seek another term. Although Rice improved the city's water supply and demonstrated that Houston's new commission form of government was more efficient than the previous city manager plan, not all Houstonians agreed with his policies. One man wrote that Rice's administration was "throwing money to the birds" and that Houston needed a mayor who would "respect authority."[7] With Rice on the way out, Houstonians were looking for change. Among civic leaders and the press, the name Ben S. Campbell kept appearing as a potential candidate. In a letter to the *Chronicle,* Judge Norman G. Kittrell said that Campbell would "give Houston a business administration" and that there would be "no retrogression" in the city's development.[8]

Campbell was a distinguished lawyer with the firm Campbell, Sewall & Myer, and many believed that his quiet, meticulous manner was just what the city needed. Initially Campbell sought to remain at his desk in private life, but, after repeated urging from friends and civic leaders, he consented to become a mayoral candidate, saying "there comes a time in every man's life when it is his duty to accept responsibility like this."[9] Campbell easily defeated his opponent and successfully served two terms from 1913 to 1917.

Campbell believed in the future of Houston, and he looked to the ship channel "as the cornerstone in building a metropolis."[10] As a city leader, he was a progressive reformer who improved public services and increased the efficiency of municipal government. He reduced Houston's floating debt of $1 million by nearly two-thirds, while at the same time creating the city's first parks and distributing the first free textbooks to schoolchildren in Texas. He also inaugurated a profit-sharing plan between the city and the Houston Lighting and Power Company and established the first civil service system. When Campbell died in 1942, an editorial in *The Houston Post* declared that "he wrought such beneficent and constructive changes in the city that older residents are prone to count time in municipal history as 'before Campbell' and 'after Campbell.'"[11]

While Ben Campbell was making good in local government, Thomas H. Ball left his law partners, Frank Andrews and Sam Streetman, to run in the 1914 Texas gubernatorial race. Backed by Progressive Prohibitionists, Ball faced the political newcomer James E. Ferguson, who held himself out as a champion of the common man. Early in the campaign it seemed that Ball would win easily, but then "Farmer Jim" countered with a negative campaign that depicted Ball as a card-playing, liquor-drinking city slicker. Despite the support of influential Texas Democrats and an implicit endorsement from President Woodrow Wilson, Ball was unable to recover from Ferguson's outrageous characterization. On Election Day, it was Ferguson who emerged triumphant. Discouraged by the intense and bitter nature of the campaign, Ball withdrew from state politics and became "one of the martyrs of prohibition."[12]

Immediately following his defeat, Ball returned to the practice of law and remained active in both the Houston and Texas Bar Associations. At the 1916 meeting of the Texas Bar Association held in Galveston, Ball supported fellow Houston attorney Frank C. Jones's successful bid for president. The following year Ball called on the Texas bar to develop "an intelligent and sane plan" for the reformation of the Texas judicial system, which Ball considered to be "the most expensive and confiscatory and cumbersome" system in the country.[13] Judge W. C. Morrow agreed with Ball but cautioned that talk alone was not enough. "You are wasting your time," said Morrow, "unless you are ready, not only to suggest the improvements and urge them through the legislature, but are also ready to go out into the press and to the public, and urge the people to pass it."[14] Judge Morrow realized that the effectiveness of any bar association was predicated on its willingness to interact with the public.

In 1917, the Texas Bar Association held its annual meeting in Houston, it being a tradition to rotate the location of the annual meeting among the major cities of the state. On July 3, Major F. Charles Hume, Sr., past president of the HBA, welcomed the state's lawyers to the thirty-sixth annual session of the Texas Bar Association. With a war raging in Europe, a strong patriotic fervor permeated the convention, which included a visit to the San Jacinto Battleground and a "real old-time Fourth of July address."[15] The convention was a resounding success and those in attendance left Houston with the conviction that the bar would do its part in America's coming trials. None of the Houston lawyers, however, could have imagined that the local bar's first battle would be in its own backyard.

As the country mobilized for war, the city of Houston faced a period of racial tension that culminated in a "night of violence" on August 23, 1917. That night, some 100 black soldiers from nearby Camp Logan, located at the present site of Memorial Park, marched into the western outskirts of Houston looking to avenge the earlier police beating of a fellow soldier. In the ensuing riot, eleven white civilians and policemen were wounded, and forty people lay dead— twenty-five policemen, two white soldiers, four black soldiers (at least one of which shot himself to avoid capture), one Hispanic civilian, and eight white civilians.[16]

While the United States Army conducted an investigation of the incident and court-martialed many of the black soldiers involved in the incident, several HBA members expressed outrage. Fearing that the military's punishment would be too light, former mayor and judge Sam H. Brashear sent a telegram to Congressman Jeff Mc-Lemore to urge "that no Negro troops be allowed to leave the city until the guilty ones are convicted and punished." To do otherwise, Brashear warned, "would have a bad moral effect in this city." [17]

Harris County District Attorney John H. Crooker wanted those soldiers under indictment for murder to be tried in Harris County. When the Army removed the soldiers to San Antonio for court-martial, Crooker and "several other prominent Houstonians" led a crusade to have the soldiers returned to Houston for trial. [18] On August 25, they held a mass meeting at the county courthouse to rally support for their cause, during which the prominent lawyer, civic leader, and former soldier Colonel Jacob F. Wolters drew loud applause when he declared that "mutiny of soldiers in time of war is treason, the penalty for which is death!" Despite the "fiery speeches," the moderates, led by Judge Robert Pleasants, defeated "the most inflammatory resolutions" and prevented an outbreak of vigilantism. [19] Two weeks later, Houston's newly inaugurated mayor, the eminent jurist Joseph C. Hutcheson, Jr., helped diffuse the situation by touring Camp Logan and affirming the Army's contention that "another riot was impossible." [20]

Although Houston's "night of violence" had ended, the violence in Europe had not. Soon American men and women answered the call to serve their country. The war disrupted the lives of many young men who aspired to build law practices. One of these men was W. B. Bates, who was graduated from the University of Texas Law School in 1915 and found himself wearing army khakis and second-lieutenant bars just two years later. During the war, Bates saw action in the Argonne Forest and was twice wounded and twice cited for gallantry. After the war, he successfully returned to civilian life and eventually became a member of the prominent law firm of Fulbright, Crooker, Freeman and Bates. [21] Another was Calvin B. Garwood, who preempted his law studies at the University of Texas in 1916 so that he could join the Texas National Guard. During the war he served in France with the 36th Division and earned the *Croix de Guerre* for gallantry in action at Belleau Wood. He remained in France until his discharge as a first lieutenant in 1919. Upon returning to the United States, he reentered the University of Texas and received his law degree in 1920. He then joined Baker & Botts and went on to become a prominent lawyer, businessman, and civic leader, as well as president of the HBA in 1935.[22] But not everyone triumphantly returned to Houston. On November 5, 1918, former attorney Captain John R. Burkett was killed in action while leading an infantry assault in the Argonne.[23]

During the war, those lawyers who were not serving in the armed forces volunteered their time and energy to the American Red Cross and the Houston War Savings Committee. Robert L. Cole, for example, served as chairman of the Red Cross Speakers Campaign, and was a member of its board of directors.[24] Some, like Robert S. Lovett, served their country as administrators in government agencies like the War Industries Board, the Allied Buying Commission, and the Capital Expenditures for American Railroads under Federal Control.[25]

When the war ended, returning service members found a vibrant city that looked to the future with optimism. Houston's war-primed economy fueled "an era of remarkable expansion" that lasted until the Depression. The rise of the corporation during this period significantly altered the face of the legal profession and put lawyers in an unparalleled position of influencing the structure of economic growth. In Houston, lawyers "served as a type of cement that bound banks, law firms, and major corporations in an alliance that fostered mutual prosperity."[26] Houston's industrial growth and economic prosperity made the city an excellent location in which to build a thriving law practice.[27]

One man looking to capitalize on the boom was Walker County Judge James A. Elkins. In 1917 he journeyed to Houston and joined the firm of Vinson & Townes, which later became Vinson, Elkins, Sweeton and Weems. Through his strong will and keen intellect, Judge Elkins became the firm's driving spirit, as well as the founder of the City National Bank. Said one lawyer: "There wasn't a man alive who could dominate anything Judge Elkins was in, except Judge Elkins."[28]

Like the previous decade, Houston's new boom brought an increase in crime and a sense of social deterioration. There was also a growing fear that "communists, anarchists, and nihilists" were infiltrating American society and that local authorities were powerless to stop them. The result was a postwar hysteria "aimed at anything that did not conform to a rigid concept of Americanism." Ostensibly to preserve American values, Houstonians organized the first official Texas chapter of the Ku Klux Klan in September 1920 and later inducted 2,051 members in a hooded, cross-burning ceremony on a prairie near Bellaire.[29]

The absence of membership lists makes it impossible to say with certainty who actually comprised Houston's Klan, but in January 1923, the *Houston Chronicle* addressed an open letter to some twenty men thought to be members. Of those named, four were members of the bar: Chester Bryan (county court judge), Murray B. Jones (district court judge), Elbert Roberts (attorney), and W. A. Cathey (attorney).[30] Contemporary HBA rosters list both Bryan and Jones as members, but there is no information available on the two attorneys.

The fact that some lawyers may have been Klansmen did not prevent other lawyers from falling victim to the Klan's terror campaign. B. I. Hobbs was a lawyer with a reputation for helping the "wrong kind" of clients—habitual lawbreakers and black people filing for divorce. On the night of February 5, 1921, Hobbs answered his front door and was greeted by four Klansmen who accosted him and threw him into the back seat of an automobile that was waiting at the corner of Prairie and La Branch streets. The assailants then blindfolded Hobbs and took him to the country, where they cut his hair off and covered his body with a thick coat of tar and feathers. After warning Hobbs to leave Houston, the Klansmen dumped him in the middle of San Jacinto Street near the Federal Building.[31]

Outraged at the growing violence, some of Houston's leaders denounced the Klan. John Henry Kirby wrote the *Houston Chronicle* that the Klan's practices were "intolerable in a free country where a government of laws under a written constitution is efficiently functioning." According to Kirby, the Klan should disband because its activities "violated constitutional guarantees of due process and trial by jury."[32] Judge Cornelius Robinson argued that "if we want tar and feathers for punishment, it is the duty of the people to write it into the laws."[33] Robinson also barred Klansmen from serving on Harris

County grand juries, but this precaution did not, of course, guarantee that justice would prevail within the courts themselves.

During the summer of 1923, the grand jury investigated a series of cases in which alleged Klansmen had beaten and whipped innocent victims in the oil town of Goose Creek, southeast of Houston. When four subpoenaed witnesses refused to cooperate with the grand jury's investigation, Judge Robinson quickly intervened. Suspecting that these witnesses were linked to the Klan, Robinson told the four men that he understood their desire not to speak out of loyalty but that "loyalty to country should be greater than loyalty to man." When the men persisted in their silence, Robinson fined them each $100 and threw them in the county jail for contempt of court. Billed by the *Post* as "one of the most sensational contempt cases in Harris County annals," the men spent eight days in jail before they agreed to cooperate with the grand jury.[34]

Although the men's testimony led to several indictments, the Klan continued to influence the justice system through the imposing persona of Judge Murray B. Jones. In a case where three Klansmen were charged with attempting to flog the Goose Creek Postmaster, Judge Jones's court ensured a quick jury verdict in favor of the defendants. Six months later, when twelve other Klansmen plead guilty "to involvement in various incidents in Goose Creek" before Judge Robinson, Jones stepped in to change the pleas of four of the Klansmen to not guilty and "dismissed their cases for lack of evidence."[35] It is paradoxical that an officer of the court who was sworn to uphold the legal rights of his constituents would seemingly associate himself with an organization that violated those very principles. Perhaps the answer lies in what motivated the Texas Klan. According to one scholar, the motivation "lay not so much in racism and nativism as in moral authoritarianism." Perhaps Judge Murray Jones, and others like him in the legal profession, viewed the Klan as a legitimate "instrument for restoring law and order and Victorian morality" in and around Houston.[36]

But not all members of the profession acquiesced to the Klan's self-appointed role of moral guardian. Concerned about undue influences in the judicial system, J. W. Lockett took the gavel as president of the HBA in 1923 and actively crusaded to raise the ethical standards of the Houston bar. Following in Lockett's footsteps,

President Hiram M. Garwood immediately called a special meeting of the board of directors to formulate an active program for the association during 1924. Meeting at the University Club, President Garwood, T. J. Lawhon, Walter E. Montieth, Lewis R. Bryan, W. O. Huggins, John G. Logue, Richard T. Fleming, and J. W. Lockett spent an afternoon discussing the problems facing the association. With lawyers linked to the Ku Klux Klan, it was imperative that the HBA evaluate its role in the profession and its responsibility to the community. Local critics of the HBA complained that it took "no steps to rid the legal profession of unworthy practitioners." Recognizing that the proper role of the association in such matters was a "debatable and undoubtedly distasteful question," the directors realized that the issue was too important to ignore. Judge Lewis R. Bryan proposed that President Garwood appoint a Committee on Legal Ethics to investigate specific complaints against members of the local bar.[37]

Although the directors unanimously adopted Judge Bryan's proposal, the HBA had limited jurisdiction in disciplining unethical conduct. As a legal body, the association had no power whatsoever to disbar an attorney. The best the HBA could do was discipline its own members by ejecting the unethical ones from the association—and even then, nothing prevented the ex-member from continuing his law practice. The inability of bar associations to "oust the shyster" had always drawn criticism from a public who charged the bar as a group with this responsibility. Astute lawyers, however, were able to use the public's low respect for the profession to their advantage by arguing that the implementation of a compulsory bar at the state level was the first prerequisite for raising standards and restoring public trust.

During the meeting the directors also organized a legislative committee to work with local legislators and the Texas Bar Association to "provide for proper representation before the legislative committees at Austin in matters in which the Bar is interested."[38]

Between 1920 and 1930, the huge expansion of the oil industry in and around Houston caused the city to experience the most rapid growth in its history. During this period, the population grew by 111 percent, from 138,276 to 292,352.[39] Across the United States, similar population growth had sparked the founding of legal-aid clinics for urban indigents. But despite Houston's growth and the concomitant problems of urbanization, the lawyers of Houston did not follow the lead of cities like New York City and Chicago in organizing a legal-aid society. In fact, when Boston attorney Reginald Heber Smith wrote his influential book *Justice and the Poor* in 1919, his research revealed that there were only forty-one legal-aid societies in the United States. Of those, only three were located in the South—Nashville, New Orleans, and Dallas.[40] The early history of legal aid in Houston is primarily one of conscientious individual attorneys doing what they could in their spare time. Although some lawyers advocated a centralized legal-aid organization, the local bar as an organization was slow to respond.

During the 1920s, both the *Houston City Directory* and the *Municipal Book of the City of Houston* listed a welfare and charity-type office called the Houston Foundation. J. W. Slaughter was the director of the Foundation, and one of the board members was Judge Sam Streetman.[41] The city of Houston created the Houston Foundation in 1915 to "advance the public welfare." In 1921, the Social Service Branch of the Houston Foundation provided assistance to 12,648 families and individuals.[42] It is uncertain whether the Houston Foundation provided legal assistance as one of its social services or if lawyers were even connected with the workings of the Foundation. Because Judge Streetman was president of the HBA in 1917 and held a position on the Houston Foundation's Board of Trustees in the 1920s, it is possible that some lawyers provided legal aid through the Foundation. The first evidence of actual HBA involvement with legal aid shows it occurring in 1924. At the February meeting of the HBA, the members discussed methods for providing free legal aid to indigent persons. The central question was whether the HBA could institute a legal-aid program under the Houston Foundation. President Hiram M. Garwood appointed a special committee consisting of Lewis H. Bryan, Thomas H. Ball, and J. W. Lockett to study the problem.[43] The HBA apparently decided against the institutionalization of free legal-aid programs.

As the national demand for oil grew and Houston's economy expanded, thousands of people, including lawyers, were drawn to the Bayou City. With an influx of new Houstonians and an already overcrowded court docket, the bar was hard pressed to meet the legal needs of Harris County. Judge Ben C. Connally recalled that Houston had the city crime that is associated with a growing city. There were "bank robbers, embezzlers, prostitution, forgers" and the like.[44] The migration of lawyers to Houston also meant an increase in the number of "shysters" and "ambulance chasers." Between overcrowded dockets and policing the seedy elements of the profession, the bar had little energy to devote to additional community services.

By mid-1925, the officers and directors of the HBA realized that they needed some type of newsletter to galvanize the bar and keep it informed of the association's activities. Under the impetus of President Richard T. Fleming, the first issue of the *Bar Association Syllabus* appeared in June 1925. To overcome the individual inertia that prevented the bar from becoming a "splendid force of benefit to itself, and to the public," the editors of the *Syllabus* urged the membership to "unite in an effort to make the Bar Association worth joining."[45] Despite the earlier discussions of legal aid and the call for greater bar participation in the HBA, one lawyer warned that the bar would become "completely moribund" unless it indulged in some activity other than "its annual banquets and its meetings memorializing its deceased members."[46]

But when the HBA attempted to do more than memorialize its dead, it ran into a heated debate. At issue was the very purpose of a bar association. In the summer of 1925, the HBA formed the Judiciary Committee to investigate the feasibility of adopting a plan relating to the selection of the judiciary in Harris County. Chaired by W. O. Huggins, the committee advocated that the HBA conduct a survey and internal election to determine which candidates to endorse collectively. At the association's September meeting, Judge J. H. Dannenbaum opposed the proposal "very vigorously" and argued that "the lawyers should take no part, other than as individual citizens in the selection of judges." W. O. Huggins countered that it was important to hold a lawyers' poll in order to "recommend to the electorate suitable candidates for judicial positions." Despite the controversy, the proposal was approved by a vote of 41 to 24.[47]

In 1926, the HBA drafted a new constitution that reflected its changing role. The inclusion of the words "to advance the science of jurisprudence" in the objectives of the HBA signified the association's commitment to promoting legal reform and education. Five standing committees were also created: Substantive Law Reform, Remedial Procedure, Legal Ethics, Membership, and American Citizenship. The promotion of "social relations between its members" continued to be a driving force within the HBA, but it occasionally went beyond the connotation of spirited fellowship over food and drink. At a meeting in January 1928, a special collection was taken up to help the widow of a former Houston attorney meet her financial obligations. The response was so favorable that $1,080 was collected when only $900 had been requested.[48]

In 1929, the debate over the HBA's role in politics surfaced once again. The issue this time was whether the HBA should adopt a resolution for the repeal of Prohibition. The outspoken Jacob F. Wolters stated that he did not believe "such controversial political issues should be injected into the Association."[49] Wolters was not alone in his belief that there were limits to a bar association's involvement. At the national level, the American Bar Association also faced criticism for its involvement in the prohibition issue. To counter the critics, a group of lawyers organized the Voluntary Committee of Lawyers in New York City and argued that for bar associations to avoid all controversial subjects was "to assert that the bar should resign its traditional leadership, since all questions involving large governmental and legal problems are subject to controversy."[50] The HBA minutes do not reveal what position the HBA ultimately adopted regarding Prohibition, but in the following years the association focused exclusively on judicial reform measures, such as creating additional judgeships to expedite Harris County's overcrowded docket.

A 1927 article in the *Houston Press* announced that the law firm of Vinson, Elkins, Sweeton & Weems believed "in young men." According to William A. Vinson, the firm wanted

> to help the young fellows. We remember that we were young once ourselves. So we try to give as many as possible a chance to make it good with us. We take on about one young chap a year. If he cuts the mustard, we advance him as rapidly as we can. We try to develop them into lawyers who will be a credit to this firm and to the bar.[51]

While Vinson & Elkins looked for men of quality, the HBA looked for ways to keep the disreputable ones out of the courtroom. Faced with the "constantly increasing number of attorneys" in Houston and the absence of any means for judges to ascertain whether "counsel appearing before them are licensed to practice law," HBA president Hugh F. Montgomery asked all members of the Harris County bar to sign a Roll of Attorneys in 1929. Such action was imperative, for one individual had already falsely represented himself as a licensed attorney before a Houston judge.[52]

Even the Depression did not curtail the flow of lawyers to Houston. Citing Houston's "steady and rapid rate of growth" and the increase in the number of practicing attorneys, David A. Simmons stated: "Obviously, there is need of a channel through which the thoughts, ideals, and opinions of such a group may be diffused to the individual members and also to the profession beyond our borders."[53] Despite the short-lived history of Richard T. Fleming's *Syllabus* in 1925, Simmons founded the *Houston Bar Journal* in late 1930. The *Houston Bar Journal* was a solid publication that focused on both HBA activities and pertinent legal issues. In a letter appearing in the Mail Box section of the March 1931 issue, one Washington, D.C., attorney wrote: "The *Houston Bar Journal* has proved very interesting reading and reflects the opinion I formed upon my visit, i.e., that the bar of Houston is splendidly representative of the vigor and life of the city and of the community of which it is a part." Ironically, the publication that Simmons created to replace the "previous spasmodic publications" of the association lasted only one year. After ten issues, the *Houston Bar Journal* also faded into oblivion; there would not be another publication of the HBA until the revival of the *Syllabus* in 1938.

Clients were harder to come by during the Depression, but there was work. According to George A. Butler, his real-estate and mortgage background helped him tremendously during the depression in doing corporate and real-estate reorganizations, of which there was a great demand.[54] J.S. Bracewell, on the other hand, became "an expert in the field of usury and tried some landmark cases dealing with tax foreclosures and collection of loans involving usurious interest."[55]

A notable characteristic of Houston during the Great Depression was the absence of a single bank failure. Thanks to the hard-nosed business acumen of Jesse H. Jones and the influence of Captain James

A. Baker, Houston did not experience the hard economic plight that hit other cities of comparable size. When two Houston banks were on the verge of failing in October 1931, Jones and Baker rallied the local bankers and orchestrated a bailout that kept the banks from closing. In 1931, Captain Baker was chairman of the board of South Texas Commercial National Bank, chairman of the Rice Institute Board of Trustees, and president of the HBA.[56]

The fact that Houston "suffered relatively less than other cities during the Depression" did not preclude some individuals and businesses from taking a hard hit.[57] Although President Montgomery had been concerned about the rapid increase in lawyers in 1929, an immediate problem in the wake of the Depression was not in obtaining legal work, but rather receiving payment for legal services rendered. Having recently moved into the new Gulf Building, the firm of Andrews, Streetman, Logue & Mobley faced a situation in which the "continued falling off" in their earnings made the monthly rental of $2,083.33 an "almost insupportable burden." To resolve the firm's "present dilemma," Sam Streetman wrote to Jesse H. Jones, the building's owner, and outlined three reasons why the managing bank should "make some concession."[58] According to Clint Morse, the firm's historian, the partners and Jones must have worked out a solution, for the firm remained in the Gulf Building until 1962.

Lawyers figured prominently in Houston's recovery from the Depression. To promote the National Recovery Act, prominent Houstonians adopted military rank and organized into "divisions." Clarence Wharton served as general chairman of the central committee and General Jacob F. Wolters was the commander-in-chief. To drum up support, Wharton challenged Houstonians to put their heart in President Roosevelt's program, because if they did not, their business was "going to the devil."[59] As mayor, Judge Walter E. Montieth formed the Unemployment Relief Committee to combat the rise in Houston's unemployment.

To guard against a future "depression," Houston's business elite began meeting informally in George R. Brown's Suite 8F at the Lamar Hotel in the late 1930s to formulate plans for Houston's political, economic, and cultural growth. Known over time as the "8F Crowd," its members included Jesse Jones, Gus Wortham, Judge James A. Elkins, and Captain James A. Baker. The shroud of secrecy surrounding the workings of the 8F Crowd makes it difficult to assess the full range of its influence, but tradition has it that virtually nothing happened in Houston without the blessing of the 8F Crowd.[60]

In October 1936, the HBA Board of Directors held a special meeting to discuss another problem facing the association, the certification of local law professors and instructors. Under the Texas Supreme Court ruling of July 1, 1936, local bar associations were required to certify that the professors and instructors of the local law schools were "fit morally, intellectually and by reason of legal attainment to guide and instruct the declarant in the pursuit of his legal study." The directors were concerned that the certificate amounted to approval for the entire course of study, when in actuality there was no assurance or guarantee that the specific standards would be adhered to throughout the declarant's schooling. Under these circumstances, President R. Wayne Lawler and the directors felt that the certificate was "too indefinite to permit conscientious action by the association with fairness to all concerned."[61]

In January 1937, Jesse Moseley and Ewing Werlein appeared before the board of directors to urge them to reverse their decision. As the president and dean, respectively, of the Houston Law School, Moseley and Werlein were fighting for the educational and legal legitimacy of their school. To resolve the problem, the board agreed to refer the matter to the Committee on Legal Education and Admission to the Bar. The next month, the committee reported its findings and advised that the teachers and instructors of the Houston Law School and the South Texas Law School be certified as being "fit morally, intellectually and by reason of legal attainments to guide and instruct the declarant in the pursuit of his legal studies." After further discussion, the directors accepted the recommendation of the committee subject to several conditions, the most significant being that the school of each declarant had to submit an annual and semiannual report of each student's progress and grades to the HBA.[62]

The next year Werlein faced another battle over the legitimacy of the Houston Law School when the Texas Bar Association's Committee on Legal Education and Admission to the Bar reaffirmed its position that a student was only eligible to take the state bar examination if he graduated from a law school approved by the

American Bar Association. In a letter of dissent, Werlein said that he was "unalterably opposed to the requirement" because it discriminated against the graduates of other law schools. Werlein believed it was ludicrous for anyone to believe seriously that the quality of legal education obtained in an approved school qualified a student to practice law any better than a school that did not have full-time professors and possessed fewer volumes of law books. Werlein was a staunch believer in improving the standards of the bar, and he believed the best way to achieve that goal was to require all students to take the state bar examination as a prerequisite to practicing in Texas. Werlein also raised the important issue of whether a private association should have the power to determine who entered a public profession. According to Werlein, only public agencies should have the authority to regulate the standards for admission to the bar.[63]

While established lawyers debated over legal education, aspiring ones were simply trying to graduate. A humorous incident involving Robert L. Cole, Jr., during his first court case illustrates that even a good legal education from the University of Texas did not cover all points of courtroom procedure. Cole recalls:

> I was present, ready, and eager to present my case at 9 a.m., the usual opening hour, and the Judge was not there. However, about 9:30 he wandered in. After 15 minutes of visiting and joking with the lawyers in the courtroom and court personnel when he still had not ascended the Bench I walked up to him and asked, 'Judge, how about us going to work?' Well, that remark beat me back to the office, because when I did return there was a note on my desk to see my father immediately. As I walked into his office, with no preliminary conversation, my father stated bluntly, 'Son, there's one thing you've got to learn—you don't talk to Judges like that!'[64]

In 1937, Lewis W. Cutrer, Arthur P. Terrell, Roland B. Voight, and other young lawyers organized the Houston Junior Bar Association to give "the young lawyers an opportunity to better know one another and to informally exchange ideas regarding the profession."[65] The members of the Junior Bar often gathered at the Grand Prize Brewery, which was close to Hughes Tool out on Houston's east side. According to Terrell, the Junior Bar "used to have real good meetings out at the Grand Prize Brewery with free barbecue supper and beer."[66] In 1930, Hugh F. Montgomery had stated that there was "no place for a senior and junior association within any locality" because the two groups needed each other to solve the problems confronting the profession. Writing in the *Bar Journal*, Montgomery said:

> My service as an officer of the Houston Bar Association has convinced me that its success is mainly attributable to the initiative and energy of its younger members. The conservatism and mature judgment of its older members is quite necessary in analyzing and tempering the enthusiasm of the younger men, but the profession must keep step with changed conditions which confront their clients. . . .[67]

If the younger lawyers were the workhorses of the HBA, they certainly were not rewarded for their efforts with prestigious positions in the association. Based on incomplete records, the average age of the HBA president from 1870 to 1922 was fifty. After the 1922 term of President John G. Logue, who, at age forty, was the youngest president of the HBA to date, the average age of the HBA's presidents until the time of Montgomery's observation jumped to sixty. These averages are a good indicator of the age of the HBA's leadership across the board, for many of the presidents served as directors or committee chairman just prior to their position as president.[68] In the 1930s, the average age began to decline, but it was still difficult for the younger members of the bar to secure leadership positions.

The late 1930s marked the beginning of the modern HBA. Through the influence of David A. Simmons at the state level and the successive administrations of Walter E. Montieth and J. S. Bracewell at the local level, major developments occurred within the association. At age 39, Simmons was the youngest man to ever serve as president of the Texas Bar Association. His charismatic personality, conviction, drive, and ability to see things in broad perspective led to innovations in the state bar that ultimately influenced developments in local bar associations. During his presidency of the state bar, Simmons created new sections for associational work, founded and edited the *Texas Bar Journal,* and established a central office.

Simmons was also very active in the American Bar Association, and in 1944 he became the youngest man in the history of the organization to serve as its president.[69]

In November 1937, Texas Bar Association President David A. Simmons addressed the members of the HBA during a dinner banquet at the Rice Hotel. Simmons stressed the need to improve the standards of the profession and said that this "may be accomplished only by well organized and coordinated bar associations."[70] At a later meeting in 1938, he related to the members how he had succeeded in having the State Bar Association maintain a central office with a permanent secretary. This development was necessary, he said, in order to give the association "some continuity of action and organized effort which had been lacking in the State Bar Association."[71] As of 1938, the HBA had no official office, but it was recognized that the secretary of the HBA desperately needed assistance in handling the growing paperwork of the association. Talk of allocating funds for an "assistant secretary" persisted throughout the year, but nothing was finalized until 1939.

It probably was no coincidence that four months after the *Texas Bar Journal* made its debut that volume two of the Houston Bar Association *Syllabus* appeared. The officers and directors viewed the publication as an essential membership recruiting tool and openly called on all "reputable lawyers of Harris County" to uphold the dignity and traditions of the profession by "engaging, wherever possible, in the activities of the Association." To achieve the lofty goal of 100% membership, the officers and directors planned to center the activities of the association "upon affairs so vital to the profession that no lawyer [could] afford to not be included in its rolls."[72]

To bolster professionalism, the HBA followed the growing national trend of bar-sponsored "legal clinics" and held Houston's first one in April 1938. The distinguished "lawyer, historian, and philosopher" Clarence Wharton delivered a colorful speech entitled "Forty Years a Member of the Houston Bar."[73] After its initial success, the legal clinic became a regular Friday-morning function in Judge Roy F. Campbell's Eightieth District courtroom.

With the success of the legal clinic, President Walter E. Montieth believed that the time was right to resurrect the issue of free legal aid in Houston. Turning to Mayor R. H. Fonville, Montieth proposed that the city establish a legal bureau to assist indigents in Houston. Mayor Fonville acknowledged that Houston indigents would benefit from such a bureau, but he stated that any legal work "would have to be done by volunteers" because the city had no funds for the proposed bureau.[74] Eager to have a legal-aid bureau of some kind established in Houston, Montieth said that there were a number of lawyers in Houston who wanted to volunteer their services. Despite Montieth's enthusiastic claim, however, the bureau never got beyond the planning stages.

Aside from the legal-aid bureau setback, 1938 was an important year for the HBA. Legal education became a priority and the constitution was amended to include twelve standing committees, one of the more important being the Committee on the State Bar Act. The HBA unanimously supported a compulsory state bar for Texas, and it created the committee to assist in the political debate taking place in Austin. Initially prepared by the Texas Bar Association in 1926, the self-governing bar bill was opposed so strongly that the Texas Legislature rejected the bill whenever it came up on the agenda. Critics of the bill claimed that it was the big-city and corporate lawyer's way of securing an unfair control over the other members of the bar. There was even concern that a compulsory association would prevent minorities from joining the legal profession.[75] Proponents of the bill countered that such allegations were unfounded and that a strong, compulsory bar was the only way to restore public confidence in the profession. Despite such claims of necessity, the legislature did not pass the State Bar Act until April 1939.

Thanks to the hard work of the Membership Committee, the HBA almost doubled in size to 343 and there was a growing sense of purpose within the association. Walter Montieth remarked: "I am told that there is at this time a better feeling of fellowship and a closer co-operation among the members of the Houston Bar Association than has ever existed before. I feel that the time is now ripe for the Houston Bar Association to take its place as the leading bar association of the entire South."[76]

Montieth's premonition was accurate, for in 1939 the HBA began a period of vigorous growth that firmly established the institutional infrastructure of today's HBA. In January 1939, J. S. Bracewell was elected president of the HBA by acclamation. However, because the newly adopted constitution stated that the president had to be elected by written ballot, former president Hugh Montgomery made a motion that a ballot be conducted "in order to avoid any question as to the election of Mr. Bracewell." Several ballots were distributed as a token gesture and promptly returned to the secretary—it came as no surprise that, for the second time, Bracewell was elected unanimously.[77]

James S. Bracewell graduated from Cumberland Law School in Lebanon, Tennessee, in June 1915. Shortly thereafter, he traveled to Harrisburg, Texas, and began the practice of law. Bracewell was politically active throughout his life and supported Walter Montieth for mayor. Bracewell's political beliefs were conservative, free-enterprise, and business oriented. His two sons, Fentress and Searcy, considered their father to be a real "go-getter" who "could not tolerate the status quo." Bracewell earned a reputation as a "fighting" lawyer who championed the causes of minorities and the criminal indigent. In 1922, when the Ku Klux Klan was "the principal political issue," Bracewell ran for district attorney as an anti-Klan candidate. Although the Klan-endorsed candidate defeated him in the election, Bracewell earned countywide recognition as a "tireless campaigner."[78]

At President Bracewell's first meeting, the board of directors approved a proposal that created a Junior Bar Section of the HBA. The Houston Junior Bar Association was in favor of merging with the senior organization and it willingly incorporated itself into the parent HBA. Director Fred Parks said that such a move "would tend to stimulate the Houston bar as a whole."[79] Although the two associations merged into one, the junior section was allowed to have its own officers and committees.

Later in the year, the HBA finally decided to employ a secretary for a trial period "not to exceed three months at a salary of $100 per month."[80] The next step was finding a place to set up a central office. At a cost of $150, the HBA remodeled a room off Judge Campbell's Eightieth District courtroom on the fourth floor of the Civil Courthouse Building and employed Mrs. Ruth Laws as the association's first secretary.[81] She successfully passed her initial "trial period" and went on to become somewhat of an institution over the years, serving as the HBA's executive secretary until her death in October 1962.

Although the HBA's first office was nothing more than "a little cubbyhole," its size did not indicate its importance to the association. For the first time in its history, the HBA had the infrastructure to coordinate its various committees and activities from year to year. Ruth Laws also took care of the daily responsibilities associated with running a bar association. She collected dues and maintained membership cards, kept records of all members and newly licensed lawyers in Houston, and disseminated information concerning bar activities to all members and the press.[82]

According to Fred Parks, a good friend and associate of J. S. Bracewell, Bracewell thought that the bar needed "to have a new charter so that it would be more democratic."[83] Bar associations across the country had consistently cried out for increased membership and the need for a more representative bar, but little progress was made. In Houston, HBA membership never included more than fifty percent of all Houston lawyers until after World War II. In 1938, for example, only 343 of Houston's 1,100 lawyers were members of the HBA. Why so small a percentage if the ultimate goal of the association was 100% local membership? Did the majority of Houston lawyers simply not want anything to do with a local bar association, or did the HBA's selection criteria intentionally limit the size and composition of its membership? Although in theory the HBA was an open membership association, the application and screening process prevented the HBA from becoming a truly egalitarian association. Like other bar associations during this period, the HBA was primarily a social organization dominated by the large law firms. Fred Parks recalls that "if the big firms had somebody they wanted as president they marched in and they voted and they marched out, and they had their president."[84]

The HBA membership in 1936 was all white and almost exclusively male. Although the 1940 U. S. Census reveals that Houston had four black attorneys, the HBA remained a segregated organization until 1965. The HBA roster for 1936 does list two women, but they may not have been practicing attorneys. The first woman was not admitted to the Texas bar until 1910; even as late as 1936, the majority of women who graduated from law school were lucky if firms hired them as legal secretaries and librarians.[85] After graduating from the University of Texas Law School, Barbara Finney went to work for Baker & Botts as a librarian, but she was fortunate enough to move up and handle a sizable amount of litigation work.[86] Said one 1925 female graduate of the University of Texas Law School: "Of course not every woman can make a lawyer. But if a girl has brains, perseverance and the will to do, she will get ahead. It's a hard row to hoe."[87] Billye N. Russell was one such woman. A graduate of the Houston Law School, she passed the bar examination in 1932 and opened a solo practice. According to Ms. Russell, it was not easy being a woman attorney.

On several occasions when I would walk in the court room and proceed to the area in front for attorneys and sit down, the Bailiff would rush over to me and say: 'I'm sorry, lady, but you will have to go to the back of the court room as these seats are only for lawyers.' When I replied, 'But I am a lawyer, Sir,' the Bailiff would take another look at the creature claiming to be a lawyer and grunt.[88]

Ms. Russell initially refused to join the HBA because every announcement of forthcoming meetings contained the word "STAG." Sometime in 1933, another woman attorney, Joyce Burg, decided that Houston's female lawyers needed their own organization. Although the women's group remained small and informal, Ms. Burg's initiative gave the women lawyers a social and professional outlet that was independent of the HBA.[89]

By 1940, Houston had twenty-one women serving as lawyers or judges. Despite a slow and steady increase in the number of practicing women lawyers in Houston, the role of women in the HBA remained limited. Women were welcomed as members, but they did not enjoy the same privilege of full participation that the male members enjoyed.

Although the HBA made major strides in advancing the legal profession in Houston by organizing its activities through an official office, the year 1939 was not without social innovations. As head of the Committee on Memorials and Good Fellowship, Ewing Werlein recommended that the association "hold some function during the summer months for the purpose of getting the lawyers together.'' The committee suggested that a golf match be held in conjunction with a barbecue and beer drinking party.[90] Werlein's recommendation gave birth to the HBA's annual barbecue and golf tournament.

Despite the HBA's goal to set up a legal-aid clinic since 1924, the Junior Bar was the driving force behind the first clinic in Houston. To ensure that the work of the clinic did not infringe on some lawyer's clientele, the Junior Bar president, Irvin H. Boarnet, wanted to exercise care in separating ''professional moochers from those really in need of aid.''[91]

As a young lawyer, Durell M. Carothers was involved in some of the Junior Bar's early *pro bono* activities. In one case, Carothers defended a man charged in Grimes County with hog theft. Despite Carothers's strong belief that his client was innocent, the court found the defendant guilty but suspended the sentence. According to Carothers:

> The memorable part of that case was that as we left the courthouse and I was downcast over having 'lost,' the defendant suggested that I drive by his wife's folks' home and he would 'give me a ham off that hog he stole.' This outraged me tremendously and I passed up the ham.[92]

In 1939 the Free Legal Aid Committee handled fifteen cases. In order to avoid controversy, the committee chairman, Lester Settegast, intentionally limited the clinic's services to cases referred to it by recognized social agencies. The Legislative Committee was also kept busy. Under Sam Neathery, the committee secured the establishment of the 127th District Court and actively opposed House Bill 288, the so called ''Winfree Bill.'' The Winfree Bill again raised the issue of whether graduates from certain law schools should be exempted from taking the state bar examination. When the HBA debated the bill in February 1939, R. Wayne Lawler declared that the standards of the legal profession ''should be as high as those of the medical profession'' and that passage of the bill ''would in no measure improve the standards, but would lower them.''[93]

In 1940, Fred Parks was chosen to head the Junior Bar section and he made it his business to develop a plan to speed up the trial of jury cases in Harris County. An April survey revealed that there were 912 jury cases, excluding divorces, on the court docket. Of that number, some 40% were more than two years old. The oldest case was filed June 18, 1917, and concerned a contract dispute over the delivery of hay to France during World War I. Apparently the case appeared on the docket year after year because a string of attorneys kept pleading that it was an active case.[94]

Despite the Junior Bar's efforts to increase the efficiency in the disposition of cases, President Parks made the mistake of answering "not ready" at a docket call on one of his cases. Aware of the Junior Bar's project to speed up the court docket, the presiding judge gave Parks and the others at docket call a stern lecture on practicing what one preaches.[95]

As war again loomed on the horizon, Houstonians kept a watchful eye and some, like Jesse E. Moseley, voluntarily returned to active military duty. As a captain in the Judge Advocate General Corps, Moseley commanded the reception center at Camp Bowie. In a letter to his colleagues on the Military Affairs Committee of the Houston Chamber of Commerce, Moseley said that he initially had some misgivings that the new recruits "from the modern and sometimes called jazz age, would not deliver the goods in a crisis," but that after a stirring graduation ceremony that included a rendition of "The Eyes of Texas Are Upon You," he felt confident that the "future destiny of America [was] in safe hands."[96]

While individuals prepared for war, the HBA took steps as a collective body to preserve the democratic way of life by joining the Inter-American Bar Association. Founded in May 1940 by representatives of twenty bar associations from thirteen North and South American countries, the Inter-American Bar Association was an organization that sought to do on an international level what bar associations had always tried to do at the national and local level. Although an internal publication claimed that the creation of the association was the "natural outcome of the steady growth of the interest of lawyers in professional associations," it was no coincidence that the Inter-American Bar Association officially organized one week after Germany invaded France. With world order again threatened, the association was a way for lawyers to unite and make an intellectual stand against international aggression.

Amidst mobilization for war and the HBA's efforts to assist lawyers in preserving their law practice while serving in the military, the directors received an anonymous complaint concerning the "divorce racket" in Houston. Apparently there was one "shyster" who went into adjacent counties and rounded up poor people who wanted to file for divorce and brought them to Houston. According to Fred Parks, a member of the HBA Grievance Committee who investigated the complaint, the biggest problem was that "technically, if somebody contested it they would not be divorced because they were not residents of Harris County." There was also a problem with a lawyer who did not even file divorce cases. He simply took his clients to the courthouse and had them wait outside until he transacted his business. "He'd come back 15 or 20 minutes later and say its been granted and here it is and he'd have it all wrapped up in red ribbon and all and charge you $25 or $30 for the damn thing and he never even filed it," says Parks. Although the lawyers in question were not disbarred, the Grievance Committee convinced the men to leave the Houston area.[97]

The success of the Grievance Committee in this situation underscored the value of the HBA's new office. In the past, Houstonians complained that the HBA did very little to protect the public from unworthy lawyers. This lack of action, coupled with a history of slow and sporadic community service, contributed to the public's perception of the HBA as a private social club. The new office, however, marked the beginning of an end to that perception. Although small and austere, the office was a place where the public could turn in time of grievance and see that the HBA was prepared to fulfill its responsibility to the community.

CHAPTER FOUR

Meeting the Needs of Society in War and Peace, 1941–1959

In the aftermath of Pearl Harbor, HBA President Murray G. Smyth used the December issue of the new *Houston Bar Bulletin* to state his philosophy as Houstonians marched off to war:

> The organized Bar has a job to do, united in the service of the nation and human freedom. We are not men of little faith, we are not weak and we are not afraid. We shall learn our duty and in the cause of liberty and justice we shall do all that is required of us and more.[1]

President Smyth's message set the tone for the HBA's role during the war years. Despite the war's disruptive effect on the legal profession, the HBA introduced services that carried over into the postwar period. Legal aid became a permanent service and the HBA recognized the value of strong public relations. The State Bar of Texas' award to the HBA for outstanding achievement in 1949 symbolized the association's growth and community contributions at a time when American values were threatened by the specter of communism.

During the war years, almost a third of all HBA members were on active military duty. Members serving in the military represented the HBA in every theater of operations. To name just a few: J. C. Hutcheson III fought in the Rhine River Crossings as a captain in a field artillery unit; Lieutenant George T. Barrow served in naval intelligence in the Southwest Pacific; Captain J. H. Freeman participated in General Douglas MacArthur's invasion of the Philippines in 1944 and also fought on Okinawa; Will Sears served under General George S. Patton; and Thad T. Hutcheson served in the navy as a lieutenant commander in antisubmarine warfare.[2]

Despite the great distances, the HBA made an effort to distribute the *Bar Bulletin* to all members in the armed forces. Throughout the war, the Service Roster was a regular feature of the *Bulletin*. It listed those members of the bar who were serving in the military and attempted to keep track of where each was stationed, thereby creating a valuable link between the front line and the home front.

With a third of the membership in the military, the collection of dues posed a problem for the directors. The dues were essential for the daily operation of the association, and their collection was imperative to the HBA's financial health. Any significant drop in revenue would necessitate a drop in bar activities and services. The directors, however, felt that it was inappropriate to expect those serving in the military to pay dues. Consequently, the HBA decided to accept any curtailment in association services necessary in order to help their brethren by waiving the collection of dues from members in the military. Cognizant of the association's "budget crunch," Percy Foreman sent the association a check for $20 to pay his bar dues for the next five years. Foreman's payment took the directors by surprise because there was no provision in the constitution for paying annual dues in advance. In the end, the treasurer took $4 for Foreman's 1942 dues and returned him a check for the balance of $16. President Ewing Werlein also wrote Foreman a letter thanking him for his support.[3]

While military service interrupted the law careers of some men, others tried to make the most of their military experience. One such man was Denman Moody. Moody originally served in the Army Air

Corps but then volunteered to join the Judge Advocate General's department and specialize in admiralty and maritime law. Moody viewed the transfer as "an excellent chance to secure a thorough course of instruction in admiralty law."[4]

Leon Jaworski resigned his position as an HBA director in July 1942 in order to go into government service. During the war he served in the Judge Advocate General Corps and achieved notoriety as investigator, prosecutor, and chief of the Army's War Crimes Branch of the European Theater. Contrary to popular belief, Jaworski did not take part in the infamous Nuremberg Trials. The notoriety he did attain resulted from the work he did prosecuting Nazi criminals during the four months preceding the Nuremberg Trials.[5]

In the summer of 1945, Jaworski's staff became the first to prosecute a war crimes trial since the adoption of the Geneva Convention in 1929. That monumental case concerned the beating and execution of eight American fliers during a prison march through the German town of Rüsselsheim in August 1944. Jaworski's investigative team pieced together the following events:

> As [the fliers] marched through the streets, a crowd gathered and began to pelt them with stones. The captured airmen tried to shield each other. They stumbled and fell. Cries of 'Beat them to death; beat them to pieces' were heard . . . Like animals, the crowd closed in. After two hours of continuous beatings, the prisoners were bloody and still. A man later identified as Joseph Hartgen, the town propaganda leader, pulled out a pistol and pumped several bullets into the mangled, lifeless bodies. Someone produced a pushcart from a nearby farm and the Americans were wheeled to the cemetery, to be buried in a common grave the next day.[6]

In the aftermath of Germany's collapse, American intelligence people found Joseph Hartgen and turned him over to Jaworski's staff for prosecution. A number of eyewitnesses cooperated with the prosecution and in the end, Hartgen was sentenced to death by hanging. Jaworski found such trials "troubling and distasteful," but he never doubted their necessity. "Our test was to be fair: to seek justice, not vengeance," said Jaworski. "I believe we met that test."[7]

When the Army offered Jaworski a position on the Nuremberg prosecution staff later that fall, he turned it down, opting instead for a discharge and prompt return to Houston. Jaworski's father was in poor health and Jaworski wanted to get home as soon as possible. There was also the nature of the Nuremberg Trials themselves. Although Jaworski believed that such tribunals were necessary, he "was concerned about their charter, particularly that part which defined an act of aggression as a war crime." To Jaworski, such a charge was *ex post facto* and he considered it "a serious mistake" to put this "new wrinkle into international law."[8]

Proud to have done his part in serving his country in time of war, it was now time to return home and serve his profession in time of peace. The lesson Jaworski took from his war crimes experience was the abuse of power, a lesson that he remembered when his country faced an abuse of presidential power twenty-eight years later.

Those not in the military were kept busy handling litigation and a variety of public services aimed at helping the war effort. In a message to the HBA, President Newton Gresham stated: "It is evident that no program or activity of any group or association can be justified in 1943 unless in some manner it furthers the winning of the war."[9] Many HBA members volunteered for service as community air-raid warden instructors, while others assisted the Selective Service in registration and draft work in Harris County. W. Carroll Barnett, Jr., for example, served as Sector Air Warden for the downtown blocks embracing the Gulf Building and Rice Hotel. Along with many other attorneys, he also assisted the draft board "in registering and counseling a multitude of draftees."[10] R. R. Lewis, an attorney and veteran of World War I, served as the coordinator of the Harris County Draft Boards. George A. Butler took time out from his new firm to serve as president of the Harris County War Chest Board.

Despite the hard work and heroics of such lawyers to fill the gap left by their brethren in the military, there were limits to what could be accomplished. The war had siphoned off some of Houston's top legal talent, leaving both individual firms and the HBA short-handed. One problem was a shortage of litigators. In Harris County, people were paying lawyers an exorbitant amount of money "to even find the courthouse, let alone if they could try a lawsuit."[11] One way to diminish the problem was to educate those lawyers who were available in the basics of litigation. To that end, the Education Committee worked hard to promote continuing legal education for lawyers and to educate the community about the work of the bar. The HBA also cooperated with the Houston medical associations and participated in an extensive venereal disease education program in 1943.[12]

Despite the shortages, hard work, and hectic pace, there were some lighter moments. In the summer of 1943 the board of directors were called upon to make a difficult decision: one Douglas McGregor demanded a refund on the tickets sold to him for the association's chicken barbecue because "the barbecue was all gone when he and friends arrived." After a short deliberation, the directors unanimously voted that no refunds be made to any Houston attorney.[13]

As the war came to a close and lawyers returned to their law practices, the HBA worked with the state bar to distribute a series of legal articles designed to acquaint those returning with the latest substantive and procedural changes in the law. Along similar lines, James L. Shepherd, Jr., recommended that the Practicing Law Institute Committee hold legal education seminars on a regular basis, saying that "no greater service can be rendered by a bar Association to its members than in providing means for study of new branches of the law . . . or developments in older branches of the law."[14] In addition to helping veterans, the HBA made arrangements "to educate the lawyers in the matter of preparing Income Tax reports so that the public [could] have the benefit of competent advice at reasonable cost."[15]

When hostilities ceased, most Houston lawyers were anxious to return to civilian life and resume practice. Dillon Anderson was "glad to have had some little part in the war" but was happy "to be back with [his] family and [his] work in the office."[16] Thad Hutcheson returned to Houston in 1946 and became a founding partner of the law firm of Hutcheson, Taliaferro & Hutcheson, which later became Hutcheson & Grundy.[17] Arthur P. Terrell was released from the Army Air Corps in November 1945 and joined the firm of Butler, Binion, Rice & Cook as a partner one month later.

The war had been disruptive for everyone and many legal careers had been put on hold. Many of Houston's present firms were started in the early postwar period as lawyers reshuffled their offices and looked for a fresh start. One such upstart firm was Bracewell & Tunks. Bert H. Tunks joined with J. S. Bracewell in early 1945, and later that year Bracewell's two sons, Fentress and Searcy, left the service and also joined the firm.[18] Searcy Bracewell recalls that lawyers in those days kept office hours on Saturday until noon because "Saturday was a big day for people to come to the city and do their shopping."[19]

George A. Butler had started his legal career with Huggins, Kayser & Liddell in 1923 and he worked for the firm for sixteen years before his entrepreneurial spirit guided him to open his own firm. In late 1941 he opened up Butler & Binion in the Gulf Building, and, just after World War II, Butler went out on a limb and hired seven lawyers returning from the war. "I didn't have the business at the time, but I did it anyway," recalled Butler.[20]

World War II was a critical point in the evolution of the legal-aid movement in the United States and in Houston. Many local bar associations, including the HBA, created special committees to handle the legal needs of military personnel. As a result, many lawyers came in contact with the reality of legal-aid work for the first time. Through their wartime experience with legal aid, these lawyers gained a greater understanding and appreciation of the legal-aid movement's purpose and benefits.[21]

The most important and active committee during the war was the Soldiers and Sailors Civil Relief Committee. The HBA established this committee to handle the legal needs of soldiers and sailors, and their relatives and beneficiaries. Through the referral of various government agencies, individuals in need were directed to the committee members, who in turn provided free advice and counsel and the drawing up of simple wills and powers of attorney. If the individual required additional legal services, the committee charged a fee commensurate with the client's ability to pay.[22] After receiving help from the committee in clearing up his marital difficulties, one sailor wrote in a letter of appreciation: "Your organization and yourself proved beyond all reasoning that there is something left in the world for me to keep on fighting for."[23]

In the HBA President's Report for 1945, James L. Shepherd, Jr., recognized the outstanding work of the Soldiers and Sailors Civil Relief Committee: "The importance of Bar Associations having available these committees of lawyers ready and willing to take care of the problems of the service man and his family cannot be overemphasized. The effect on the morale of the men in the service was tremendous.'' While the Soldiers and Sailors Civil Relief Committee handled about seventy cases per month, the Committee on Free Legal Aid received few calls from civilians. Shepherd attributed this to the ''large number of people who had close relatives in the armed forces and to the small amount of unemployment during the war.''[24]

At the close of World War II, ABA President David A. Simmons commended all members of the bar for a job well done, but he cautioned that ''it would be negligence on our part to allow this organization for legal assistance to die down without having something to put in its place.''[25] Lawyers across the country heeded President Simmons's call. In 1940, there were sixty-three Legal Aid Offices in the United States. By 1949, the number of offices had increased to ninety-two.[26]

The Junior Bar had been engaged in *pro bono* work since the late 1930s but Houston did not have an official legal-aid clinic. The HBA's creation of the Free Legal Aid Committee in 1941 was the first step in making such a clinic a reality. The war interrupted the establishment of a clinic, but the work of the Soldiers and Sailors Relief Committee largely performed the same service. After the war, the Free Legal Aid Committee returned to studying the problem of opening a clinic. In August 1948, Curtiss Brown, chairman of the committee, met with the board of directors and delivered the committee's recommendation that the HBA establish a Free Legal Aid Clinic in Houston. Director Herman Pressler agreed and made the motion that the board of directors approve the committee's recommendation and submit it to the membership for a general vote. The board believed that it was important to act now because some other organization not responsible to the bar would meet the demand for a Free Legal Aid Clinic if the bar did not.[27]

In Houston, twelve years after Walter Montieth's 1938 proposal, a legal-aid bureau finally came to fruition. Federal Circuit Judge Joseph C. Hutcheson, Jr., was the driving force behind the clinic. He believed that Houston had ''long lagged behind in providing this service for its poor people'' and that it was time for the local bar to fulfill its professional responsibility.[28] As a federal circuit judge, he commanded the respect of the legal community and he used his position to build support for a legal clinic.

HBA President Nowlin Randolph supported Judge Hutcheson by making the establishment of a legal-aid clinic the HBA's major project for 1948. To ensure maximum support for the clinic, the HBA conducted an advisory poll of its membership. After the past several abortive attempts at establishing a clinic, the membership's decision to sponsor the clinic by a vote of ten to one was a pleasant surprise.[29] The creation of a legal office where the poor of Houston could actually visit was an important step in attaining equal justice for all. As one official put it, the HBA's Free Legal Aid Committee "just wandered about aimlessly" prior to the clinic's organization.[30]

The Houston oil entrepreneur and philanthropist Hugh Roy Cullen donated $15,000 to help establish and fund the Legal Aid Clinic's first year of operation.[31] To manage the Legal Aid Clinic's operating budget, the HBA organized the Houston Legal Foundation in 1948 as a charitable, nonprofit corporation under the laws of the State of Texas. Despite the HBA's overwhelming approval of the Legal Aid Clinic, not all Houston lawyers were in favor of its operation. According to Judge Hutcheson, some of the younger and less established lawyers "had the idea that a legal aid clinic would interfere with their obtaining and building a practice."[32] These lawyers did not prevent the HBA from establishing the Legal Aid Clinic, but their active protest indicated that the livelihood of some lawyers depended on the low-income clientele that the clinic proposed to serve. In 1948, these lawyers were too few in number and poorly organized to pose a serious threat to the HBA's plans for a legal-aid clinic.

Houston was the first city in Texas to operate a legal clinic with a full-time director. Under the guidance of Sam T. Cook, the Legal Aid Clinic handled approximately 300 cases in its first six months of operation. In his annual report for 1949, HBA President Leon Jaworski praised the work of the Legal Aid Clinic, saying that its work was of the "utmost importance" to the legal profession. "Free services performed by lawyers individually to needy clients seldom reach the ears of the public; a sizable fee, be it ever so reasonable, always does," stated Jaworski. "It is only through the medium of a body such as the Legal Aid Clinic that our assistance to the needy unable to pay for services will come adequately to the attention of the public.''[33] The State Bar of Texas also noted the exemplary work of the Legal Aid Clinic and selected the HBA for the 1949 Award of Merit for "the most outstanding and constructive work accomplished" by any association having a membership in excess of fifty.[34]

During the 1950s, the Legal Aid Clinic continued to grow in size and importance. With the assistance of students from the Law School of the University of Houston, the clinic handled 1,446 legal problems in 1950. Almost half of the cases processed involved family problems such as divorce, child support, and adoption. After the clinic exhausted Hugh Roy Cullen's $15,000 donation, the Houston Community Chest Council and the United Fund provided the necessary monetary support. The operating budget of the clinic in 1952 was $12,500.[35] During the period 1948 to 1963, the Legal Aid Clinic and its successor, the Legal Aid Society, handled more than 26,000 cases.[36]

In Texas—as well as in the rest of the United States—the lawyers' greatest fear in the 1950s was that the United States government would "socialize" the legal profession in order to meet the growing need for legal aid. To assess the status of legal aid in Texas, the directors of the State Bar of Texas conducted a 2,062-mile "Legal Tour" of the state and introduced a systematic approach to meeting the needs of Texas' indigent through the "Texas Plan."[37] Whereas Houston's accomplishments in legal aid had lagged behind other comparably sized cities prior to World War II, Houston began to develop a different image. The city of Birmingham, for example, had no legal-aid service whatsoever—despite having a population of 300,000. In New Orleans, the legal-aid office handled about 600 cases a year, while the Legal Aid Clinic in Houston handled about 1,000 cases annually.[38]

Just as legal aid flourished in the postwar period, so did the role of women in the HBA. With the help of President Palmer Hutcheson, women attorneys organized a Women's Section in 1947 and selected Sadie Gough, Norma Bemus, and Mary Francis Hickman officers. Once the section was organized, women became more active in the various bar committees, though their numbers remained small because there were few women lawyers in Houston. In 1947, for example, the HBA had sixteen committees with a total of 136 members. Of that 136, only two were women—Joyce Burg and Isabel Breit.[39]

That same year the San Antonio Bar Association petitioned the HBA to form its own women's auxiliary. To organize such a body, Palmer Hutcheson requested the help of Junior Bar President Reagan Cartwright and Virginia Noel. The initial role of the Women's Auxiliary was to assist the HBA in connection with social functions, including the state bar convention to be held in Houston in July 1948. Two years later the auxiliary sponsored the first annual fall Harvest Party, a major social event that continues to this day. Over the years the auxiliary grew in size and expanded its objectives to include community service projects that promoted "a better understanding and relationship between the general public and the legal profession."[40]

Both the Women's Section and the Women's Auxiliary facilitated the appearance of women in increasingly greater positions of responsibility within the HBA. In 1949, Billye N. Russell became the first woman to run for a position on the HBA Board of Directors. Although she lost to Denman Moody, Ms. Russell's candidacy set the stage for Wilminor Carl's victory two years later. Wilminor Carl came from a family of lawyers and was graduated from the University of Texas Law School in 1929. In 1950 she served as chairman of the Women's Section and in 1951 she became the first woman ever to serve on the board of directors of the HBA.[41]

In early 1946, the HBA had 1,069 members. To accommodate a membership of this size, the HBA held its meetings in the 113th District Court because it was the largest courtroom in Houston. The primary concern of the new president, Earl Cox, was the creation of a trust fund for indigent lawyers and their families. A proposal was put before the entire HBA and approved in April. To create the trust fund, membership dues were increased to $6, and the board of directors was authorized to select "some" Houston bank as the custodian and trustee. The method used to select the bank was surprisingly arbitrary: the name was drawn from a hat![42]

The creation of the trust fund represented the HBA's commitment to expanding services for its members. Another significant service was the Harris County Law Library. Under the energetic leadership of William L. Kemper, the Harris County Law Library Committee prepared the first catalog ever of the publications available in the library and distributed a copy to every lawyer in the county.

Although the HBA initially emphasized services to its members as a means of generating lawyer interest in the association after the war, the presidents of the late 1940s and early 1950s began to place a greater emphasis on community service and public relations. The public took notice of the HBA's efforts in providing community services, and soon the HBA was overwhelmed with special requests. In March 1948 two Army officers asked the HBA to sponsor a counterintelligence unit. The rationale behind the Army's request is not known, but the board of directors promptly turned it down. In January 1949 the HBA received a letter requesting that the association help bring about changes in the "setup of the Houston Independent School District." The directors discussed the issue and concluded that "this matter did not follow within the functions of the bar." And in June 1949 the HBA turned down a request for funds by Texas State University's new law school, citing that the HBA was not in a position to make gifts. Despite the HBA's commitment to serving the public good, there were limits to the type of projects it could undertake.

When Herman Pressler became president in 1950, he wanted the HBA to emphasize public relations and activities that were of direct service to the community. To promote public relations, the HBA created the Public Relations Committee and appointed W. S. Jacobs, Jr., and Norman J. Bering chairmen. Realizing that public relations was multifaceted, Jacobs and Bering divided their committee into five sections: Speakers' Bureau, Bank and Trust Company Publications, Public Relations Survey, Fellowship and Liaison with Press and Radio, and Selection of Public Relations Counsel. Although the committee made substantial progress in outlining a broad public-relations program, the lack of funds prevented the implementation of a full-scale program. Because of budget constraints, the committee's activities were limited to what its volunteer members could accomplish. The Speakers Bureau furnished speakers on the National Vocational Guidance Panel to Houston's high schools and other civic and service clubs. The committee also furnished judges for debate competitions and distributed copies of the *Bar Bulletin* to all the newspapers within 100 miles of Houston.[43]

Those HBA activities having the greatest impact on the community were in the areas of free legal aid. Along similar lines was a proposal for a lawyer referral service where Houstonians "could call and be referred to lawyers who would register with the service and indicate their willingness to have referrals made to them." Some lawyers, however, argued that such a service would reduce their clientele and drive them out of business. Others claimed that a referral service violated the profession's traditional disdain for lawyer advertising. Herman Pressler tried to rally support by warning: "If we do not ourselves fill this need, then we will find governmental planners moving in and taking over in this field."[44] Pressler's warning failed to resolve the controversy and the directors put the referral plan on hold.

Pressler had much greater success in providing assistance to servicemen who were called up during the Korean War. Due to the increase in enlistments and inductions, the HBA reactivated the Armed Services Relief Committee to "handle free of charge the legal problems of service men, particularly those problems incident to arranging their business affairs prior to entering the armed forces."[45] In conjunction with other programs, this expanded service necessitated an increase in membership dues. For the first time in its history, the HBA introduced a scaled dues schedule based on a given member's number of years in the profession. Those lawyers practicing less than five years paid $6 and everyone else paid $10.[46]

The Korean War, however, was not the only perceived threat to American security. On the home front, Senator Joe McCarthy's national attack on communism helped fuel Houston's own "Red Scare."[47] An editorial in *The Houston Post* predicted that "the people will generally approve" of the American Bar Association's recent declaration that "no one who is presently a Communist is fit or should be permitted to be a member of the bar."[48] Like other institutions and organizations of the day, the HBA had its own anticommunist oath written into its constitution as a condition to membership. As of 1951, the HBA Constitution proclaimed that members of the Communist Party were ineligible for membership. In 1953 the HBA Bar Committee rejected one lawyer's application to practice before the United States District Court for the Southern District of Texas because of that individual's association with another lawyer suspected of being a member of the Communist Party. Citing the adverse Bar Committee report, District Court Judges Thomas M. Kennerly, Allen B. Hannay, and Ben Connally denied the application. The Fifth Circuit upheld their decision on procedural grounds, but the United States Supreme Court later found "no sufficient grounds for the failure and refusal of the District Court to grant petitioner's application for admission to the bar of that court," and reversed the decision in 1955.[49]

By 1950 there were 2,044 lawyers in Harris County. Of that number, 1,250 were members of the HBA. The remaining 794 were not members for a variety of reasons, but some were denied access because of their skin color and personal ideology. The anticommunist oath kept some away, but the explicit constitutional provision that applicants had to be "white" blatantly violated the HBA's long-standing goal of 100% lawyer participation. T. Everton Kennerly recalls:

> The colored lawyers weren't given very good treatment, and I remember at the library they had them segregated on a certain table. We tried to do away with that and we helped a little, but it took two or three years before that injustice was changed.[50]

It took a lot longer to admit black lawyers as members. A motion to strike the word "white" from the constitution "died" on the table during the 1952 annual meeting. While the HBA debated the integration issue over the next fourteen years, the black lawyers of Houston formed their own professional organization called the Houston Lawyers Association.[51]

In 1951, T. Everton Kennerly ran for president as a candidate from a "small law firm." Kennerly won the election; he later recalled the association's "unwritten tradition" of rotating presidents among the various sectors of the legal community:

> The Bar was composed then a lot like it is now. Big law firms, small law firms, independent lawyers, and lawyers in legal departments. And it was sort of a custom to take one from each category each year so as not to have the big law firms getting all the Presidents or create any dissension and it worked out very well.[52]

Kennerly was from a small law firm, whereas his predecessor, Herman Pressler, was from the Humble Oil legal department. The following year Harry R. Jones from Andrews & Kurth was elected president. It is not known how far back this tradition goes, but a cursory look at the list of the past presidents reveals a discernible pattern by 1917 whereby Andrews & Kurth and Baker & Botts had a president every few years. In 1949 Fulbright & Jaworski became a regular member of the rotational circuit when Leon Jaworski served as president.

When President Kennerly presented his annual report to the association in 1952, he concluded his report with five recommendations: 1) expand the Grievance Committee of the State Bar for the Eighth Congressional District; 2) continue and expand the work of the American Citizenship Committee; 3) compile a pictorial roster of the individual members; 4) consider the possibility of installing officers in July rather than in January in order to conform to the State Bar of Texas' election of officers; and 5) continue the Harvest Party as an annual social event.[53] The American Bar Journal applauded Kennerly's progressive outlook in an editorial, "A President's Finest Hour." The journal said:

> In all the country, only one outgoing president devoted his annual address to specific observations and recommendations for his association's future work, culled from that year's activities and experience . . . T. Everton Kennerly thus appraised the past and future of his association to the lasting profit of its members, many of whom could in no other way learn definitely what had been and what should be done and why. A program sold to the members will succeed.[54]

Another active committee during 1951 was the American Citizenship Committee chaired by Vic Gould and W. Carloss Morris, Jr. Originally created in 1926, the HBA now promoted this committee as an answer "in these critical times to the many 'isms' besetting our community." Believing that it was the lawyers' duty to take the lead in promoting citizenship, the committee used the media to educate Houstonians on the responsibilities, obligations, and duties of a good

American citizen. The American Citizenship program grew to such an extent that both the State Bar of Texas and the American Bar Association adopted some of the HBA's ideas.[55]

When Paul Strong became president in 1953, he placed emphasis on establishing a separate domestic relations court and five additional civil district courts for Harris County. *The Houston Post* said that Harris County's "galloping population has probably overrun more cow pastures in the past 10 years than any other domain its size in the United States" and that its citizens were "facing what amounts to a denial of justice" because of the county's insufficient number of courts. Whereas across the country the average was one court for every 50,000 people, in 1953 Houston had only one court for every 92,400. The case backlog was so bad that Paul Strong told the *Post* that a man was "lucky if he can get a contested case to trial in two years."[56] The problem was that the legislature was not creating new courts fast enough to keep pace with the volume of litigation arising from Houston's growing population, urban development, and increased industrialization.

While the HBA tackled the court problem, Vic Gould and the American Citizenship Committee continued to expand the scope of their program. At the suggestion of the committee, Mayor Roy Hofheinz issued an official proclamation designating February 25, 1953, as "Open House at City Hall Day."[57] While the goal of the HBA was to acquaint Houstonians with the functions and problems of their government, the underlying message was preserve the "American Way of Life." That summer an incident flared up that tested the city's conviction to defend that way of life.

According to historian Don E. Carleton, leftist activism had been a visible part of Houston life since the 1930s. Houston's postwar "frenzy of growth" propelled the city into "the metropolitan stage of development," and, like the societal costs of Houston's post–World War I economic boom, this growth served as a catalyst to motivate those acting as "guardians of democracy." The Korean War and McCarthyism further legitimized the credibility of Houston's Red Scare activists. Even the issue of land use zoning in Houston sparked a heated public debate that borrowed from anti-Communist rhetoric. Those against zoning claimed that zoning was "un-American" and a "threat to the American Way of Life."[58]

One of those opponents was Ewing Werlein. According to Carleton, Werlein "was among the most vocal of those Houstonians subscribing to the view that Communism posed an immediate danger to the local citizenry." After serving as HBA president in 1942, Werlein became president of the Houston School Board in 1948 and openly "attacked federal aid to education, claiming it would end initiative and individuality."[59]

In 1952, the conservatives on the school board believed that Houston School District Superintendent Bill Moreland was "ideologically undependable" and that he should be replaced. The board, however, agreed to give Moreland another chance "to prove himself" and they allowed Moreland to hire a deputy superintendent as an assistant. For deputy superintendent, Moreland selected George Ebey, an educator from Portland, Oregon, to serve a one-year contract. The fact that Ebey was an "outsider" and an advocate of "progressive education" did not work to his advantage when it came time for the school board to renew his contract. Houston's Red Scare activists accused Ebey of being a communist sympathizer and a promoter of racial integration.

Faced with a full-scale hearing, George Ebey hired Jack Binion, a name partner with the firm Butler, Binion, Rice & Cook, as counsel. Binion also served on the State Board of Education and his background allowed him "to identify with his client's predicament." Despite Ebey's unpopularity and alleged communist affiliation, Binion offered his services "because [Ebey] was entitled to counsel." When Ebey asked Binion about the lawyer's fees, Binion replied, "You don't owe me one red cent, podner."[60]

In a closed meeting with the school board, Binion argued that Ebey's offense of "being controversial" was "a new type of delinquency in American life." According to Binion, the issue "is whether a man falsely accused . . . is to be punished for having been an innocent victim of a situation he did not create."[61] When it came to the final vote in an open session before a packed audience, the school board voted 4 to 3 not to rehire Ebey.

The George W. Ebey affair was the high point of Red Scare activism in Houston. By the fall of 1953, an increasing number of

Houstonians began "to speak out against the witch-hunt in the city."[62] Although the HBA never played a formal role in the affair, some of its prominent members appeared on both sides of the debate. As lawyers, both Jack Binion and Ewing Werlein were dedicated to preserving the liberties that the profession was sworn to protect. Jack Binion represented the moderate element within the bar. Ewing Werlein's staunch conservatism represented the extreme end of lawyer involvement. Although Werlein "was a man of unshakeable conviction," he was dedicated to the Houston bar and, above all, to the civic affairs of Houston.[63] His anticommunist views were devoted to the preservation of the democratic freedoms he so dearly loved.

As an association, the HBA eventually dropped its anticommunist oath. However, in keeping with the tradition of the lawyer as constitutional guardian, the HBA retained a clause in its own constitution that banned members who advocated the overthrow of the government.

Several years later, the HBA made a more substantive change to its constitution. Since its inception as an organization, the election and inauguration of officers had always coincided with the new calendar year, but in 1957 the directors changed that tradition. Implementing an earlier recommendation by past president T. Everton Kennerly, the directors voted to install new officers in July, in order to have greater continuity with the state bar. William N. Bonner's administration was the first to serve under the new system.

As in the past, success in the HBA continued to be an excellent stepping stone to positions of greater responsibility. After serving as HBA president in 1945, James L. Shepherd, Jr., went on to serve as the president of the state bar in 1946–1947. As president of the state bar, Shepherd emphasized the participation of lawyers in both the state and local bar associations. He also helped to establish "a close and cooperative relationship between the judiciary and the practicing lawyers."[64] In 1957 Shepherd was named chairman of the ABA House of Delegates.

After serving as president of the HBA in 1943, Newton Gresham also later served as president of the state bar in 1956–1957. A strong believer in the role of bar associations as a catalyst for greater professionalism, Gresham visited lawyers in the smaller cities and towns throughout Texas in order to promote the value of the state bar as a professional organization.[65]

In 1955 Lewis W. Cutrer served as president of the HBA and two years later successfully ran for mayor against incumbent Oscar F. Holcombe. A close associate of Walter E. Montieth, Cutrer became interested in politics when Montieth was elected mayor in 1929. Thanks to Montieth, Cutrer served as an assistant city attorney while his friend was mayor. Always an opponent of Oscar F. Holcombe, Cutrer had had to quit his job as assistant city attorney when Holcombe defeated Montieth in 1933. Apart from his law practice, Cutrer spent the next twenty-five years in and out of public office, depending on whether Oscar Holcombe was the presiding mayor.[66]

When a political scandal weakened Holcombe's administration in 1957, Cutrer decided to run against his old nemesis. Cutrer served three terms as mayor and made significant contributions to alleviate Houston's growing pains. In 1958 Houston lacked an adequate industrial water supply to support the growing industrial complex along the Houston Ship Channel. The solution was to divert water from the Trinity River, but there was one major obstacle—the Trinity River Authority. According to one historian, the Trinity River Authority "was a Dallas-oriented agency and was charged with being generally disinterested in helping Houston solve its water problem."[67] To win support for Houston's cause, Cutrer waged a vigorous public-relations campaign in the counties along the Trinity River. The hard work paid off and in September 1959 the city of Houston and the Trinity River Authority signed an agreement that gave Houston "a supply of water estimated to permit expansion up to the year 2010."[68]

Cutrer also helped to alleviate Houston's air transportation problems by closing a deal to purchase 3,125 acres of land on Houston's north side for the construction of an airport capable of handling the airlines' new jet aircraft. During his administration, Cutrer hired professional planners to design the new facility and secured new air routes from the Civil Aviation Board. Although Cutrer was no longer in office when Houston Intercontinental opened in 1969, his earlier policies and support made the airport a reality.[69]

Although the challenges of urban expansion and the problems of city government consumed most of his time, Mayor Cutrer never forgot his legal roots. In 1958 he enthusiastically endorsed the American Bar Association's plan and President Dwight D. Eisenhower's proclamation establishing May 1 of each year as "LAW DAY." Speaking from City Hall, Cutrer said:

> It is this liberty and equality for the individual which distinguishes our system of government from communism, under which millions of people are today living in slavery. Without laws and courts the freedoms we often take for granted would be meaningless. This important truth is to be recognized publicly in a nation-wide observance of Law Day U.S.A. to be held on May 1, 1958. All American citizens have been invited to participate.[70]

With the support of Mayor Cutrer, the HBA took the initiative in sponsoring Law Day programs in Houston.

By 1959 there was growing support among Houston lawyers to build a professional center much like the Dallas Bar Association had built. Of all the Texas bar associations, only Dallas had a club-type headquarters. A special HBA committee chaired by William N. Bonner felt that if Dallas could do it, so could Houston. According to Bonner, his committee found that a bar headquarters or center was

> a strong influence in the respective communities where such headquarters are in operation, in unifying the Bar, giving direction to its public service activities, and in promoting the cause of continuing legal education.[71]

President Joyce Cox made the bar center his top priority, but he found that planning a bar center and actually constructing it were two different things altogether.

Writing in the *Houston Bulletin,* Cox asked whether the bar was "now willing fully to accept [its] professional responsibilities and privileges?" Citing the impressive response of local schoolchildren to the HBA's Constitution Week Essay Contest, Cox further stressed the importance of lawyers providing leadership in the community:

> The children's response brings to mind the need of all our fellow citizens for that leadership which has heretofore come and in the future can come from the Bar alone. This thought should cause

us to center our energies more in our profession; for if the salt of the earth should lose her savor, wherewith will it be salted?[72]

Cox was obviously trying to drum up support for the upcoming membership vote on the proposal for the new bar center. To make the plan a reality, no less than 55% of the membership had to affirmatively approve in writing such a center and promise cooperation in its operation.

By 1959 there were close to 1,800 members of the HBA, but there were still some 600 to 700 Houston lawyers who were not members. With an estimated price tag of $100,000, the HBA wanted maximum participation in order to reduce the individual burden to each lawyer. Apart from the constitutional limitations on membership applicants, the HBA admitted that "many non-members [had] refrained from participating in Bar activities because they say the Bar Association has no meaning."[73]

The Houston Bar Center Advisory Committee recommended that the lawyers raise the money themselves, stating: "We have a feeling that our professionalism does not mean much to us if we are not able to raise an average of $75 from each of at least 1,500 lawyers in the city of Houston."[74] Although a formal membership vote showed that 73% favored a bar center, the actual financial responses were dismal. The critical element was money.

Faced with inadequate funding, President Cox conceded that the timing was not right for such an endeavor. But Cox also expressed dismay over the bar's lack of support for the project:

> Encouraging as our progress is, we are still far behind what is done in Dallas and other cities where the profession has a true home for its functions. It is not conceivable that the greatest Bar of Texas, in the most populous city of the South, lawful guardians of the tradition of liberty under law, should be either unable or unwilling to provide the facilities for their own professional effectiveness.[75]

Throughout the spring of 1960, Cox used the *Houston Bar Bulletin* to reiterate that the purpose of the new bar center was for professional activities. Apparently annoyed at persistent rumors to the contrary, he stated: "I should like to correct emphatically and for the last time an unkind rumor that has been circulated to the effect that the Bar Center will be principally a drinking place."[76] Regardless of Cox's refutation of such rumors, funding continued to be a problem.

As a break from the frustrations of bar center politics, Cox instigated the association's first shipboard legal institute. In April, members enjoyed a seven-day cruise to Jamaica and the Grand Cayman aboard the *M. S. Italia.* James Kronzer fondly recalls that the trip was "the first real week of cohesiveness the bar ever had" and that it "made the bar more homogeneous."[77]

When Cox turned the president's gavel over to Kraft Eidman, the project that he had started and worked so hard for was incomplete. Despite this setback, Joyce Cox raised the bar's level of awareness of its responsibility to the community. He was a man of vision who realized that changing times demanded fresh approaches. Cox served at the critical time when the individualism of the past was waning in the face of rising social activism and egalitarianism. Although the Houston bar was slow to "adjust itself to this fact of existence," Cox was optimistic that the "increase of interest and activity" during the year promised well for the future of the organized profession.[78] Cox was right.

CHAPTER FIVE

Expansion and Innovation, 1960–1972

President Kraft Eidman thought it was appropriate to begin the new decade with a reflection on the objectives of the association. With Houston ranked sixth nationally in population, Eidman believed that the bar would be faced with additional opportunities and obligations. After ninety years, the objectives were little different from those that guided the early founders of the HBA:

1. Advance the science of jurisprudence.
2. Promote and facilitate the due administration of justice.
3. Advance the standing of the legal profession.
4. Preserve and enforce the ethics of the legal profession.
5. Encourage social relations between its members.[1]

At no previous time in the history of the HBA did the association come closer to fulfilling its objectives. The legal and social climate for reform in the 1960s, coupled with a string of exceptional presidents, accounted for the HBA's success in pioneering new programs.

Before the HBA could expand services to the community, the association had to first address its own needs. To ensure that the association would "always have continuity of vigorous policy and

104

action,'' the HBA created the position of ''president-elect.''[2] Latimer Murfee was the first member to fill that position, serving from July 1960 to June 1961. The most pressing need, however, was new office space.

In December 1962, Chairman John H. Crooker, Jr., of the Bar and Headquarters Committee formally presented his committee's recommendation for the location of a new HBA office. The first choice was the Houston Club Building, and the second choice was the Rice Hotel. Because the HBA often held meetings and social gatherings at the Houston Club, the directors unanimously selected the Houston Club over the Rice Hotel. The new HBA office had 460 square feet and cost $185 per month.[3] According to President Hall E. Timanus, the HBA moved out of the courthouse because ''the committee . . . felt that the association needed to grow and in view of the fact that Mrs. Laws was stepping down—it was an end of an era—it was time for us to move out of the courthouse and go on our own, so to speak.''[4]

By the early 1960s, photocopying machines began to transform daily law office duties. Until then, manual typewriters and costly and tedious reproduction procedures kept the copying of documents to a minimum. Only a handful of stores offered photocopying—Ridgways was a favorite among lawyers.[5] Some law offices did have a crude form of document reproduction: ''We had some sort of duplicating machine at the firm that you ran something through and it would come out wet. You'd hang it on a wire and if you let it get into the sunshine it would fade out,'' recalls Clint Morse.[6] The Xerox revolution did as much to revolutionize the legal profession in the 1960s as the computer revolution would do in the 1980s.

Friday mornings at the courthouse were ''sort of a social call for all the trial lawyers.'' Hartford Prewett recalls that at docket call you would ''always see somebody dressed very casually in a loud sport coat'' that would trigger a round of joking. ''Hey, it's your docket call outfit that you have on there; surely you wouldn't be selecting a jury dressed like that!''[7] Despite the jovial atmosphere, a sense of inequality tainted the serious side of business. When it came to setting the docket, a hierarchy existed that depended on race. Judge Carl Walker, Jr., recalls: ''Black lawyers who were representing clients would be last on the docket to be heard. A white lawyer representing a black client would be next to the last to be heard. A white lawyer with a white client would be the first—regardless of when you got there."[8]

As a young assistant district attorney in the early 1960s, Carl Walker, Jr., petitioned the HBA to strike the word "white" from its constitution. On at least one occasion, says Walker, an HBA president told him to "just wait until my term is up."[9] There was a degree of reluctance on the part of some lawyers to tackle the problem head on and make change occur. George T. Barrow, however, did not shy away from the problem.

As president, Barrow submitted a proposal in 1964 that called for deleting the word "white" from Article II, Section I, of the HBA Constitution. The Constitution and By-Laws Committee studied and endorsed the proposal, but when it came time to vote, the membership rejected the proposed change. Barrow later recalled: "I really can't understand and I can't say why it failed, but the bar association refused to adopt the resolution which I had prepared to integrate the HBA."[10] Although Barrow considered the proposal's rejection to be the primary disappointment of his tenure as bar president, his commitment to racial equality and willingness to debate the need for change ultimately contributed to the proposal's passage one year later.

When W. James Kronzer became president in 1965, his first order of business was also to remove the "white only" clause from the HBA constitution. Kronzer felt that such racism "was ridiculous for professional people" and held an emergency board of directors meeting that "went on all day and well into the night. We just stayed in that directors room up at the Houston Club . . . and concluded to finally take it out," says Kronzer. No record was kept of the discussion so that "everybody got to speak their voice."[11] Once the directors agreed to delete "white" from the constitution they presented a referendum to the membership. This time, however, the HBA voted 1,097 to 321 to admit blacks as members.[12]

Although Kronzer was "very proud of the result," the majority of Houston's forty black lawyers did not rush to join the HBA. The feeling among black attorneys was that integration did not necessarily mean full participation. Because of that, many black lawyers decided to remain in their own association—the Houston Lawyers Association—where they were guaranteed prestigious committee positions.[13]

If the failure of desegregation was George Barrow's biggest disappointment, his greatest success was in transforming the *Houston Bar Bulletin* into *The Houston Lawyer*. The *Bulletin* had always been "a reporting organ" that kept the membership current on the association's latest activities. Although the *Bulletin* presented some substantive issues in the form of committee reports, Barrow believed that it could be much more. "I envisioned that *The Houston Lawyer* should be a publication which would in time become a real, honest-to-goodness periodical and would contain articles to carry on a continuing legal education."[14] Barrow had the idea, but it was Quinnan Hodges who had the plan. Editor of his college publication, Hodges brought both experience and creativity to the task of producing a periodical that "lawyers in Houston [could] profit by so reading."[15] The first issue of *The Houston Lawyer* appeared in November 1963.

That same month the HBA participated for the first time in the Pre-Release Program. Concerned about the high percentage of inmates released from the Texas Prison System who were returning to the department of corrections, Dr. Beto of the Texas Department of Corrections developed a "Pre-Release Program" to educate inmates prior to their return to normal life. The five-week program covered a wide range of topics, and a number of local businesses and agencies donated time to cover their area of expertise. A special HBA committee, chaired by Guy Nevill and Charles Saunders, presented lectures on the lawyer's role in society and addressed any legal questions that the inmates had. The program was a great success and was responsible for cutting the number of released prisoners who ended up in prison again.[16]

In August 1965, the American Bar Association awarded the HBA Honorable Mention for outstanding and continuing work in the field of commemorating Law Day U.S.A. This honor marked the first time that the HBA received an award from the American Bar Association.[17] Working with the local federal judges, the American Citizenship Committee conceived the idea of having a naturalization ceremony on Law Day. Held in the Music Hall, this ceremony soon became a Law Day tradition.

The HBA faced a new dimension to the legal-aid problem in the early 1960s—the issue of criminal defense for the indigent. Despite a poor tradition of civil legal aid in Texas, Texas did provide legal aid for the indigent in criminal cases. The Sixth Amendment to the United States Constitution said that the accused was entitled "to have the assistance of counsel for his defense." In Texas, the civil statutes allowed district and county judges to appoint counsel to those who were too poor to employ counsel.[18] Before 1963, the judge made the final ruling on whether a criminal was indigent and entitled to counsel at the government's expense. Unless the criminal was accused of a capital offense, the judge could always deny counsel. However, in 1963 the United States Supreme Court decision in *Gideon v. Wainwright* assured the criminal's right to counsel. In *Gideon*, the United States Supreme Court ruled that states had to provide counsel for indigents in criminal cases regardless of the offense.[19] This meant that even those accused of misdemeanors were entitled to counsel. In the early 1960s, there were not enough Houston lawyers available who were sufficiently skilled in criminal work to handle the new influx of cases that were likely to arise from the *Gideon* decision. Thomas M. Phillips resolved to implement a program to meet this need during his tenure as president of the HBA during 1964–65.

Work on an indigent defense plan had begun in 1963 under President George T. Barrow. Barrow appointed Fred Parks to head a committee of some twenty-five lawyers to develop a workable plan. Through the hard work of committee members such as John Maginnis, R. Gordon Gooch, and Myron Sheinfeld and the cooperation of Judge John R. Brown and Judge Ben C. Connally, the leading lawyers of Houston studied the problem of indigent criminal defense for two years before acting on the *Gideon* decision.[20] In forming its criminal program, the HBA leadership adhered to the principle that "anyone who cannot afford to pay for legal services must have the same opportunity for justice as one who can."[21] The HBA's final plan was the first of its kind in the United States to employ a fully coordinated "assigned-counsel system" involving the city's entire legal profession. In essence, Houston's 3,500 lawyers were put on a master list and were notified when it was their turn to represent a defendant.

The HBA revamped the old Houston Legal Foundation (HLF) and made it the managing agency of the Houston Defender Program, Legal Aid Society, and Lawyer Referral Service. The funding for the criminal branch of the HLF came from a $375,000 Ford Foundation grant and donations from the M. D. Anderson Foundation, the Brown Foundation, and Houston Endowment, Inc. To assist the indigent in civil cases, the HLF received a $704,486 federal grant from the Office of Economic Opportunity's Legal Services Program as part of the War on Poverty.[22] Associate Justice Tom C. Clark of the United States Supreme Court presided over the formal dedication ceremony of the Houston Legal Foundation's new offices in the Houston First Savings Building, at Fannin and Capitol on March 12, 1966. Justice Clark praised the Houston National Defender Program and predicted that it would become a pattern for other cities: ''I know of no other program in this field that has the coverage of yours.''[23]

The implementation of the Houston Defender Program was the first time that the voluntary HBA had ever made lawyer participation mandatory. Traditionally, lawyer involvement had centered on joining a committee and working in a specific area. Because of its mandatory nature, not all lawyers endorsed the plan. According to Thomas Phillips, ''Many lawyers did not want to give up their time, and understandably so. But as long as we could present it as a situation where every lawyer was serving no more than his just time and all lawyers were contributing, it met with the approval of the vast majority of the lawyers.''[24] The program ultimately succeeded because the leading lawyers and judges of Houston strongly supported the program.

To administrate this ''novel experiment,'' Phillips brought in Judge Sam D. Johnson of the 66th Judicial District in Hillsboro to serve as director of the HLF. When asked why he would resign his judgeship to become the director of the HLF, Johnson replied, ''Although my lifelong ambition has been to be a judge, the opportunity to become a part of the new and great program initiated by the lawyers of Houston could not be passed up. It is the first program of its kind in the country, and the ideal of 'Equal Justice Under Law' shall be achieved.''[25]

Under the HLF system, even the most hardened criminals received first-rate legal representation. Phillips says: ''In the course of representing these indigents, we provided them some of the best—and highest priced—legal service that they ever had. And we turned them loose. I'm not proud to say we turned them loose because of that fine representation . . . . But they got their day in court and they were well served."[26]

Not only were criminals turned loose, but prosecuting attorneys were challenged by some of Houston's finest trial lawyers. Kronzer recalls one incident involving Leon Jaworski: "Colonel Jaworski. . . got assigned a case involving some alleged criminal and he had three of his young people with notebooks and all ready to go. And finally the DA said, 'Man, I can't handle this. I quit.'"[27]

Trouble began for the HLF when it sought funding from the Office of Economic Opportunity (OEO) for the Civil Division. Prior to 1966, the HLF's indigent defender program and lawyer referral service were independent local organizations. The fact that the HLF had a successfully functioning legal services program that was strongly supported by the HBA leadership made it "an excellent vehicle for the OEO to use in bringing bar support behind a program of civil legal services on a massive scale."[28] To the HLF, OEO funding represented an opportunity to expand services in the civil area of law. The problem was that the OEO insisted upon representation of the poor on the board of trustees, a condition that the HLF would not accept. For most of the trustees, there "was never any question about the matter: laymen were not going to run this legal services program."[29] In fact, some of the trustees even admitted to what the critics already suspected—that the HLF only expanded into the civil field "to prevent legal services in Houston from falling into the hands of laymen in general and social workers in particular."[30]

Thanks to the negotiating skills of R. Gordon Gooch, the HLF resolved its differences with the OEO by creating a district board that answered to the board of trustees. The district board coordinated services at the neighborhood level and was open to minorities and the indigent.

The success of the Civil Division had an unintended effect on the Lawyer Referral Service. Before the HLF organized the Civil Division, the Referral Service "was strictly a bar association operation." Its primary purpose was to make the services of local attorneys available to Houstonians who had no contact with attorneys. Some indigents did call, but those who used the service were largely middle class. When the Referral Service merged with the Civil Division, it "was given the additional function of referring gray-line indigency cases." The result was that middle-class clients stopped calling the Lawyer Referral Service because of its identification with the HLF. This in turn caused some lawyers to drop out of the program because there was less chance of getting a good fee-producing case. Realizing that declining participation in the Lawyer Referral Service had an adverse effect on the bar's ability to meet the legal needs of all citizens, the HBA and HLF moved to a system of telephone referrals.[31]

Through the Lawyer Referral Service, Houstonians could call and make an appointment for $1 to discuss their problem with a qualified lawyer. Under the program, lawyers charged only $10 for a full hour of advice. Houstonians utilized the Lawyer Referral Service for a variety of purposes. The following quotes are examples that appeared in the December 1969 issue of *The Houston Lawyer*:

Woman: "My toilet has been plugged up for 3 days. What should I do?"

Gentleman: "I've got a problem and I don't know how to handle it. My attorney obtained a very substantial judgment for me and now won't take any fee."

Politician: "My lawyer says that 'Legal Ethics' preclude him from contributing to my campaign. Is that right?"

Man: "I don't want no lawyer. I just want to know the name of a good laxative."

Mr. X: "Can you get my attorney to answer his phone?"

Despite the early success of the HLF, there was opposition to the Office of Economic Opportunity's Legal Services Program in Houston from the beginning. Some lawyers did not want a government agency intervening in the legal affairs of Houston. Individual practitioners were especially concerned that their poorer clientele would make use of the indigent services, thereby robbing them of income. In 1948, the Free Legal Aid Clinic had faced opposition from a small body of "young lawyers." In 1966, the HLF faced determined opposition from a new organization called the Texas Society of Practicing Lawyers, Inc. (TSPL). The TSPL's membership claimed that it was an "organization dedicated to safeguarding the economic interest of the individual attorney."[32] The president of the TSPL, J. Charles Whitfield, Jr., argued that it was critical that the HLF establish clearly defined standards of indigency; otherwise, the government-funded HLF would drive the individual attorney out of business. Throughout the late 1960s, the TSPL challenged the legality of the HLF in a series of court battles—and lost.

In *Touchy v. Houston Legal Foundation*, the plaintiffs—consisting of individual attorneys and the Texas Society of Practicing Lawyers, Inc.—claimed that the HLF was a corporation engaged in the practice of law in violation of Article 320a-1 of the Texas Revised Civil Statutes.[33] The HLF countered with a motion for summary judgment and plea in abatement during a hearing in the 165th Judicial District Court of Judge Thomas J. Stovall, Jr., on February 20, 1967. Representing the HLF were trustees Leroy Jeffers and Curtiss Brown. They argued that the courts and the bar had a responsibility to provide legal services to the poor and that the rendering of such services fell within the specific authorization of Canon 32 of the Texas Canons of Ethics, which read in part: "The professional services rendered of a member shall not be controlled or exploited by a lay agency, personal or corporate, which intervenes between client and a member. . . . Charitable societies rendering aid to the indigent are not deemed such intermediaries."[34]

After considering the pleadings and argument of counsel for both parties, Judge Stovall granted the motion for summary judgment and plea in abatement in favor of the HLF. Judge Stovall based his decision on two grounds. First, that the prohibition against the practice of law by a corporation did not apply to charitable societies rendering aid to the indigent by virtue of the exemption provided in Canon 32. Second, that the appropriate action in the case of an alleged ethics violation by a member of the state bar was to initiate proceedings through the state bar's accepted grievance procedures and not through an original action in the district court.[35]

Not willing to give up easily, the TSPL petitioned the Court of Civil Appeals for a rehearing. Once again, the court found in favor of the HLF. One year later, however, the Supreme Court of Texas reversed the Court of Appeals and ordered that the cause be reinstated on the docket of the 165th Judicial District Court of Harris County for a trial on the merits. According to the Supreme Court, the trial court "did not reach the merits" because it held that the petitioners did not have standing to maintain the suit. The Supreme Court held that "due to the special interest attorneys have in their profession, they have standing to maintain a suit to enjoin action which allegedly damages their profession."[36] By the time the case came to trial, the HLF had fallen on hard economic times and was forced to curtail services. The HLF's funding difficulties convinced the TSPL that another challenge was unnecessary after the TSPL lost on appeal in *Scruggs v. Houston Legal Foundation*.[37]

In 1967 the board of trustees of the Houston Legal Foundation invited the University of Houston Law School to conduct an intensive three-month evaluation of the foundation's operations with a view toward publication of both the strengths and weaknesses of the program. The results of the study appeared in the *Houston Law Review* in May 1969, and the final verdict received mixed reviews. The primary criticism was that the HLF was only "a modern and enlarged version of a legal aid society" and not a true legal services program that took on controversial cases to engineer social change through litigation.[38] To buttress their arguments, the critics pointed to the HLF's handling of the Davis case.

The substantive issue in the Davis case was school integration. Mrs. Melvyn Davis wished to enroll her son in a segregated class of a partially integrated school. When school authorities refused to admit her son, she turned to the HLF for help. The HLF initially took her case, but open opposition from the TSPL soon forced the HLF to reconsider its position. The TSPL charged that Mrs. Davis was not indigent "because her divorced husband could have been required to contribute to their son's legal expenses." After investigating their claim, Sam Johnson agreed and withdrew the HLF from the case. Some Houstonians, however, regarded the withdrawal as "a flimsy and insincere pretext for avoiding controversy."[39] The position of the HLF Board of Trustees was that it was inappropriate for the HLF to "get involved in political issues, stir things up, or try to change the world."[40] In essence, the HLF was a legal-aid society that was geared toward giving every person a day in court. It was never the purpose of the HLF to lead a crusade for social change and civil rights. President J. Charles Whitfield, Jr., of the TSPL was quite pleased with the HLF's withdrawal from the Davis case. He categorized Mrs. Davis's suit as "a test case by the civil rights groups to see if they can get a free ride off the Federal Government."[41]

One evaluator concluded the HLF was less effective than it ought to be because the HBA only set up the program to prevent other groups, such as black lawyers and social workers, from establishing a true legal services program that might erode the HBA's influence and control. The evaluator criticized the HBA's motives, saying that the HLF's policy of "a self-perpetuating board of 'lawyers only' ha[d] the effect of excluding lay people, poor people, and representatives of the poor from having a say and a vote in policy matters, thus contravening the federal antipoverty policy of 'maximum participation' by the poor, for the poor."[42] One proponent on the evaluating team, however, presented a realistic appraisal of the HLF's predicament:

> Given the Houston dislike for federally funded programs and a segment of the local bar so opposed to the HLF that it established a separate organization which challenged the validity of the HLF in the courts, it would have been foolhardy to engage in aggressive programs in order to achieve short-run goals only to be rejected by the community in the long run.[43]

Despite the critics, the HLF made every effort to meet the needs of Houston's indigent. The agency's central office was located downtown in the Houston First Savings Building and housed the director, the chief of the Civil Division, the program evaluator, the Lawyer Referral Service, and offices for staff attorneys. Strategically located in "selected poverty pockets throughout Harris County" were nine neighborhood offices that gave the indigent a place to seek legal recourse. In the first eleven months of operation, the HLF helped 3,587 clients and established a reputation as having "one of the best legal services programs in the nation."[44]

In 1966, the American Bar Association held its annual convention in Montreal, Canada. Fifty years after Reginald Heber Smith conducted his classic study of legal aid in the United States, the American Bar Association's highest honor went to the Houston Bar Association—a bar association that had no legal-aid program at the time of Smith's study.

Reflecting on the association's accomplishments during his tenure as president, Thomas Phillips said that the hard work and collective effort of the Houston Legal Foundation "really elevated the legal profession in the eyes of the community."[45] Phillips's statement was not a self-serving accolade, for one Houston newspaper echoed his sentiments: "The community has reason to be proud of having a progressive bar association that has blazed the way by making justice available to all regardless of financial circumstances."[46]

Contrary to popular belief, lawyers have not always commanded extravagant legal fees. In fact, before the HBA established a legal-aid clinic for the indigent, it created a special fund for indigent lawyers. Each lawyer or firm seemed to have its own system of calculating fees and charging clients. Searcy Bracewell wrote:

On the last day of each month late in the afternoon, we got together in the conference room and would talk about who should be billed and how much it should be. There were no such things as time records. One of us would jot down on a yellow legal pad the bills which we thought should be sent out and how much they should be. This list would be turned over to a secretary to prepare the bills. I'm sure we forgot a lot of charges we should have made and, of course, generally forgot the time spent on a matter. During these sessions, we would have arguments over how much to charge a client . . . . It never really occurred to any of us to log the time which had been involved.[47]

Some lawyers considered it unprofessional to send a client a bill unless the client asked for one. When queried about billing a client, Homer Mabry of Andrews & Kurth replied, "I haven't sunk to sending bills yet!" A stance like the one taken by Mabry did mean that some legal work went unpaid, but for the most part, the good clients asked for a bill or simply paid what they considered a fair price.[48]

In 1966, the HBA published a Recommended Minimum Fee Schedule to help lawyers set reasonable fees. The Bar Economics Committee, chaired by George B. Strong and Tom Arnold, dedicated the fee schedule "to the concepts that adequate legal fees will ensure adequate legal representation and that only through financial soundness can the Bar continue the availability and effectiveness of its services." An American Bar Association publication called "The 1958 Lawyer and His 1938 Dollar" pointed out that a lawyer had only 1,300 "fee-earning" hours per year and that approximately 40 percent of every dollar of gross income was needed to pay the overhead of operating a law office.[49] A sampling of the listed fees includes: office consultation, $30 per hour; corporate organization, $250; depositions, $30 per hour; uncontested divorce, $250 to $350 depending on number of children and amount of property; simple will, $50; oil and gas lease, $50; general partnership agreement, $250; limited partnership agreement, $350; probate of the estate, 3% of gross estate value; contingent fee contracts, 33 1/3% of recovered amount; ordinary misdemeanor tried in county criminal court, $250; capital felony, $1,500.[50]

The Bar Economic Committee also stressed that the keeping of accurate time records was "indispensable to the full utilization of this fee schedule."[51] As the legal profession moved toward a more systematic approach to fees, the lawyer's major administrative concern became "billable hours." For many lawyers who began practicing before the 1960s, this change took the fun out of legal practice. According to Arthur P. Terrell, "The aspect of law which has changed the most . . . is the manner of keeping time records and the manner of billing. I think it has taken a lot of pleasure out of practicing law but I believe it is necessary due to the great overhead of a lawyer at this time."[52]

Like most lawyers, the colorful Percy Foreman based his fees on a "mystical compromise" between the HBA's recommendation and what he thought the traffic would bear. What set Foreman apart, however, was his willingness to accept unusual forms of payment. In an interview with the *Houston Chronicle* Foreman said, "I prefer cash, but if a client hasn't got any I'll take anything of value that he does have—excepting his home, if he's a married man.'' As a result of his barter system, Foreman accumulated a collection of automobiles, real estate, jewelry, furniture, and household appliances.[53]

In the mid-1960s the HBA took a hard look at meeting the future legal needs of Harris County and hired an architectural firm to develop a long-range courthouse building program. In 1965, Harris County had fourteen civil district, six criminal district, and four domestic relations courts. Given Houston's rapid population growth, the civil district courts already had a backlog of 33,361 cases. With a population of approximately 1.5 million, Houston was five courts short of meeting the ABA's longtime recommended standard of one court for every 50,000 people. Even if that standard were met, Judge Thomas J. Stovall, Jr., said that ''it would take the courts about three years to overcome that backlog.''[54] The HBA favored legislation that would create at least three new district courts and a second court of civil appeals in Harris County in 1967. In addition to these new courts, an HBA committee headed by Spurgeon Bell recommended that the commissioners court call an election for a bond issue to finance construction of a $3.6 million Family Law Center. The initiative for a Family Law Center was the first time that the HBA had developed and instigated such a bond issue. *The Houston Post* supported the HBA's plan for the Family Law Center and called on Houstonians to vote ''yes'' in the upcoming election.

On March 27, 1967, groundbreaking ceremonies were held for the new Family Law Center. It was the hope of HBA President Arthur P. Terrell that the new center would ''remind each of us to remember always the importance of *The Family* as a strong unit.''[55] Prior to the Family Law Center, the domestic relations courts were scattered across town and were often in ''shoddy locations.'' Judge William M. Hatten told the press that the courts were ''operating in facilities that the smallest country town doesn't operate in today.''[56] Judge Hatten, for example, presided in a makeshift courtroom in the shoddy old former city police station, where sirens often disrupted proceedings when fire engines pulled out of the fire station located downstairs.

During 1967, the HBA also began work on establishing a new administrative office. The officers and directors made arrangements with Houston Endowment, Inc., to name the new Rusk Building at the northeast corner of Rusk and Main Streets the "Houston Bar Center Building." The plans called for both the bar offices and a restaurant and club to occupy the second floor. In a letter to the association, the Bar Center Committee stressed that for the HBA "to grow and to remain healthy," the need for a bar center was "obligatory." It was imperative that the HBA have its own home. "Up to now our Bar Association has been dependent on the bounty of the County or upon the generosity of the Houston Club for a home. As a result, we have been 'camping out'—first a cubby hole in the old Courthouse, then a larger cubby hole in the same remodeled building, and then nice but inadequate space with the Houston Club."[57]

The Houston Club Building had been an interim step on the way to building a grand bar headquarters in the vision of Joyce Cox. The opening of the Houston Bar Center Building in 1968 capped a long period of dreaming, planning, and hard work. Housed in the center were the HBA's administrative offices, lounge facilities, and the new Inns of Court Club.[58] The one-time initiation fee for the Inns of Court Club was $25 for lawyers having practiced five years and under, $50 from five to ten years, and $100 for more than ten years.[59]

In its first years of operation, the Inns of Court Club was a liability for the HBA. Lawyers did not use the club with the regularity required to operate at a profit. Another problem was that the cost of establishing the Houston Bar Center and the Inns of Court Club had exceeded the estimates of contractors by some $37,000 and no one knew why. None of the minutes reflected that the board of directors had ever authorized the expenditure of funds to cover the additional costs. Working with the Bank of Texas loan officers, HBA Treasurer Burke Holman was able to secure a loan for the association that covered the additional costs and expenditures.[60]

The HBA and the Inns of Court Club were not the only ones confronted with a budget crisis. By 1970, the Ford Foundation's five-year pilot program for funding the HLF had almost run out. This development forced HLF Director Thomas M. Roberson to go looking for funds. In March the commissioners court tentatively agreed to finance the HLF's program to aid indigent criminals, but it did not officially authorize funds until one week before the HLF was planning to shut down its criminal division. Once again the TSPL smelled blood and stepped up its attack on the HLF. One TSPL member accused the HLF of "high-priced muddling" and suggested that volunteer law students and clerks be used to interview prisoners and brief the law. HBA President W. Ervin "Red" James countered with a warning: "If you abolish the Houston Legal Foundation you will have lost forever a vehicle you might possibly not want to cast aside."[61] James was right. The HLF was a "vehicle" for providing services. Without some type of organizational framework and coordinating body, even the TSPL's alternative plan to use law students and clerks would be impossible.

In 1971, Henry McCormick replaced Roberson as director of the HLF, which became the Gulf Coast Legal Foundation the following year. At a testimonial luncheon in 1977, Gulf Coast Legal Foundation officials honored Henry McCormick as the man who "did nothing less than keep the beleaguered agency alive through its most difficult period." McCormick tried to downplay his accomplishment, but he did admit that "things were pretty grim." Not only did the TSPL continue to challenge the HLF on ethics questions through litigation, but President Richard Nixon's administration drastically curtailed funding of the Office of Economic Opportunity's Legal Services Program. "I can remember times when the day before payroll was due, there was no money," recalled McCormick. "But the staff went ahead with their primary obligation—helping those without any money at all." In 1971, McCormick had to scrounge for funds through the local agency of the OEO, an agency that was highly critical of the HLF's lack of effort in engineering social change. Fortunately McCormick was able to make peace with the local agency and secure the necessary funding.[62]

On May 21, 1971, the HBA celebrated its 100th anniversary with a special centennial dinner at the Astroworld Hotel. In 100 years, the HBA had grown in size from 100 lawyers to more than 2,800 members. But more importantly, the HBA was a vital part of the Houston community. President Royce R. Till presided over an elegant black-tie banquet, which featured introductory remarks from ABA President-elect Leon Jaworski and an address from Chief Justice Robert W. Calvert of the Texas Supreme Court. Chief Justice Calvert paid high honor to the HBA and to those "who organized and have sustained it." Calvert, however, tempered his praise of the association and Texas jurisprudence with a word of caution: "We still have problems to solve; and a chronicle of the glories of the past or a mere indulgence in self-praise, with eyes closed to our deficiencies, will not suffice."[63]

Hartford Prewett listened to Chief Justice Calvert that night, and when he became president of the HBA the following year, Prewett sought to analyze where the association was headed. Stressing the importance of formulating "an idea," Prewett stated:

Someone once said that 'The little mind talks about people, the average mind talks about events, but the wise mind talks about ideas.' It is my feeling that herein lies the key. Before we can have any worthwhile program, we must first come up with an idea—we must then have the dedication and courage to launch the program and see that the goals are attained.[64]

To formulate that idea, Prewett held a special meeting of the board of directors at the Quail Creek Country Club in Hempstead on Saturday, October 30, 1971. In an all-day session, the directors discussed the issues facing the HBA and tried to make "an in-depth study of what the aims, objectives and goals of the [association] should be" and the best way to accomplish them. The consensus born out of the meeting at Quail Creek was that it was "high time that the Houston Bar Association moved forward with less timidity and became more actively involved in areas of social change and service to the community."[65]

During the meeting, the directors discussed the role of the association in judicial evaluations. The problem in Houston was that not all lawyers and judges believed that such activity fell within the sphere of a bar association and there were concerns over prejudicial evaluations. The directors decided to submit a referendum to the entire membership on whether the HBA should evaluate the performance of the Harris County judiciary on an annual basis and make the results publicly known through the media.[66] Objectivity was a key concern, but as long as the evaluations were fair, they were a great help to voters. If lawyers were not qualified to evaluate the judiciary, then who was?

A more sensitive issue the directors considered was the role of the HBA regarding controversial matters within the community. With 2,800 members with as many potential viewpoints, any official HBA position on a given issue was bound to spark controversy within the association itself, let alone in the local community. Was it even the role of the HBA to take an official position on controversial matters? Some of the directors believed not and advocated that the HBA should merely inform the public that there was an issue that demanded public attention. The role of the HBA was to point out the "pertinent questions concerning the issue." Others felt that the membership should be polled on whether or not the board of directors should take a stand on matters of community concern. After due discussion, they adopted the following resolution:

Resolved, that the Houston Bar Association should and will become more involved with public issues, controversial or non-controversial, and the Board of Directors will take a stand on such issue as each arises.[67]

In April 1972, the HBA had the opportunity to demonstrate its commitment to increased involvement in controversial public issues. Larry Thompson, in the capacity of liaison between the Junior Bar and a coalition of local environmental groups, was interested in obtaining an HBA endorsement for a comprehensive mass transit plan. After some discussion, the board of directors decided that "mass transit" was beyond the long-standing policy of the board to confine its actions to matters concerning the judiciary and the profession.[68] Although the directors' decision contradicted the Quail Creek resolution for greater community involvement, the HBA did pursue mainstream social service programs, and these efforts garnered the praise of Leon Jaworski.

In 1971, Jaworski became the second HBA member to serve as president of the American Bar Association.[69] Upon becoming president of the ABA, Leon Jaworski sent a letter to his "colleagues of the Houston Bar Association." Jaworski thanked the membership for their support and applauded them for outstanding achievement. His comments are a fitting testimony to a decade of expansion and innovation.

What gives me the greatest sense of pride as I visit our nation's Bar Associations, both local and State, is the rightful opportunity of pointing to the stature of my own Bar Association. Your achievements have won awards and recognitions on numerous occasions, of which all of us are justly proud. In my view, there is no Bar group that is greater—there is none that is grander.[70]

The Big Three: Thomas M. Phillips, W. James Kronzer, and George T. Barrow, from left to right. Beginning with Barrow in 1963, these three men served consecutively as president of the HBA and were responsible for the success of the Houston Legal Foundation.

The Houston Legal Foundation opens for business. From left, Judge Sam D. Johnson, Justice Tom C. Clark, Thomas M. Phillips, and W. James Kronzer at the dedication ceremony on March 12, 1966. Courtesy of the Houston Chronicle.

Theodore Voorhees, President of the National Legal Aid and Defender Association (second from left), presents the Harrison Tweed Award to (left to right) W. James Kronzer, immediate past president of the HBA, Judge Sam D. Johnson, executive director of the Houston Legal Foundation, and Arthur P. Terrell, president of the HBA.

When it came to legal fees, the colorful Percy Foreman preferred cash but would accept "anything of value." Courtesy Houston Metropolitan Research Center, Houston Public Library.

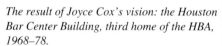

The result of Joyce Cox's vision: the Houston Bar Center Building, third home of the HBA, 1968–78.

Houston lawyers and judges relax at the new Inns of Court Club at 713 Main shortly after it opened in 1968.

Leroy Jeffers, Judge George Cire, and County Commissioner "Squatty" Lyons share a lighter moment at the Dedication Ceremony for the new Family Law Center.

Hartford H. Prewett, 1971–72 HBA President. His special meeting at the Quail Creek Country Club laid the foundation for expanded HBA community service projects.

One of the HBA's most distinguished members: Leon Jaworski.

Past presidents of the Houston Bar Association. First row seated and kneeling, from left: Royce R. Till, Leon Jaworski, Newton Gresham, Joyce Cox, Leroy Jeffers. Second row seated: Hall E. Timanus, Latimer Murfee. Third row standing: Hartford H. Prewett, Harry R. Jones, Lewis W. Cutrer, William N. Bonner, George T. Barrow, Arthur P. Terrell, Paul Strong, Harry W. Patterson, Kraft W. Eidman, Thomas M. Phillips, Hon. W. Ervin James.

Attorney Sybil Balasco, left, chats with Carl F. Mann, Jr., after a C.L.E. seminar on construction financing in 1969.

Charles Keilin (right) and Firmin Hickey, Jr., (center) were the driving force behind the HBA's pioneering CLE programs. Here Keilin congratulates moderator Joe Draughn on a successful Probate Institute.

The Houston Bar Association Officers and Directors for 1973–1974. Front row, from left: Seaborn Eastland, Jr., immediate past president, Vincent W. Rehmet, president, Ralph S. Carrigan, president-elect. Second row, from left: James B. Sales, treasurer, W. Scott Red, secretary, Hon. Nancy Westerfeld, second vice president, Charles R. (Bob) Dunn, director. Third row, from left: John L. McConn, director, Bill Pravel, first vice president, John O'Quinn, director, Harold Lloyd, director, Al Taylor, director. Judge Westerfeld was the second woman to serve on the HBA Board of Directors.

The HBA helped arrange a mass investiture ceremony at the Houston Music Hall when the Harris County juvenile and domestic relations judges officially became district judges in 1977. Several new criminal district courts were also created that year. Pictured back row, from left: Judges Wallace H. Miller, Robert Lowry, Criss Cole, Wells Stewart, Herman Mead, Allen Daggett, William Elliott, Felix Salazar. Front row, from left: Judges Jimmy James, Sam Emison, Henry Schuble, John Peavy, Bruce Wettman, Richard Millard.

In 1979 the HBA moved to its fourth home, the Texas Commerce Bank Building.

The two presidents who led the HBA into the 1980s. Left: Charles R. (Bob) Dunn, 1979–80. Right: James B. Sales, 1980–81.

Described as "the pivotal factor in the growth and prosperity of the association," Kay Sim has been the HBA's Executive Director since 1981.

John J. Eikenburg's administration demonstrated that "Lawyers Care" and that they know how to have fun.

129

The HBA celebrated the sesquicentennial of the Texas judiciary with the mock trial of a Texas hog farmer found guilty of larceny in 1836. Upper left: Witness Rufus Wallingford of Fulbright & Jaworski, retired District Judge Thomas Stovall, Jr., and Jimmie Lee Rush, 55th District Court reporter, listen attentively. Upper right: Harris County Sheriff Johnny Klevenhagen holds attorney Michael Gallagher in custody as his weeping mother, retired 11th District Court clerk Betty Turner, offers sympathy. Lower left: Former 11th District Judge William Blanton, Jr., 263rd District Judge Charles Hearn, Harris County District Attorney John Holmes, and retired District Judge Thomas Stovall, Jr., pose for admirers. Lower right: The Texas Barflies provided down-home entertainment. They are from left, Max Addison, Diana Marshall, Prof. David Crump, special guest Judge Sam Alfano, and Judge David Hittner.)

Past presidents of the Houston Bar Association. Back row, from left: Charles R. (Bob) Dunn, James B. Sales, Albert B. Kimball, Jr., John J. Eikenburg, Hon. Joe L. Draughn, James Greenwood III, George E. Pletcher, Ralph S. Carrigan, Seaborn Eastland, Jr., Hartford H. Prewett, Tom Arnold, John L. McConn, William Key Wilde, Harry W. Patterson. Front row, from left: Kraft W. Eidman, George T. Barrow, Herman Pressler, Denman Moody, Thomas M. Phillips, Newton Gresham, T. Everton Kennerly, Hall E. Timanus, Arthur P. Terrell, Frank B. Davis.

John J. Eikenburg, left, and Ewing Werlein, Jr., release the results of an HBA Judicial Evaluation Poll to the media.

HBA President Raymond C. Kerr and "The People's Lawyer," Richard M. Alderman, hand out awards at the 1988 annual Law Week Fun Run, benefitting the Center for the Retarded, Inc.

THE houston lawyer
March-April 1989   Vol. 26 No. 5

**Can Professionalism
Prevail Over 'Rambo'?**

*The deterioration of lawyer
professionalism and the rise of
"Ramboism" in the 1980s seriously
tainted the legal profession's public
image. Photo copyright Chris
Kuhlman Photography.*

*President Ewing Werlein, Jr., faced
the timeless problem of restoring the
"dignity of the profession."*

As president, Justice Eugene A. Cook had the HBA Mandate on Professionalism printed and distributed to every lawyer and judge in Harris County. Justice Cook also was the architect of "The Texas Lawyer's Creed—A Mandate for Professionalism."

The guardian of HBA tradition: President Pearson Grimes, 1990–91.

First City Tower is the fifth, and present, home of the HBA. Ewing Werlein, Jr., was instrumental in the acquisition and development of the new offices.

On May 1, 1991, the Harris County Historical Commission, the HBA, and the law firm of Butler & Binion dedicated an Official Texas Historical Marker to commemorate the history of the HBA. Located in front of the Harris County Civil Courts Building, the marker was prepared and donated by Butler & Binion on its 50th anniversary. Pictured is F. Russell Kendall, vice chair of the HCHC and attorney with Vinson & Elkins. Photography by Gaylon Wampler. Copyright The Houston Post.

The HBA is committed to serving the community through programs such as: LegalLine (upper left), Juvenile Mock Trial (upper right), Ask the Expert (lower left), Coat Drive for the Homeless (lower right).

135

Justice Eugene Cook completes the Fun Run with a special friend from the Center for the Retarded, Inc.

Susan Soussan and husband-and-wife attorneys Roger A. Rider and Nancy Huston enjoy the annual Harvest Party at the River Oaks Country Club.

Husband-and-wife attorneys Thomas J. Brandt and Susan Brandt at the Harvest Party.

Former HBA President Harold Metts presents HBA President Ben L. Aderholt with five portraits of former association presidents from Baker & Botts. Courtesy of Rick Gardner.

Attending the HBA's annual luncheon for Houston area bar leaders are, from left: David Fraga, Berta Mejia, Kathleen Gasner, Otway B. Denny, Jr., (HBA President 1992–93), and Jose Cantu.

Secretary of State James A. Baker III, former partner of Andrews & Kurth.

CHAPTER SIX

A Mandate for Professionalism, 1973–1990

According to one legal scholar, Watergate "raised the most profound and tormenting questions about the ethics and values of the legal profession."[1] The legal profession across the country reeled from the large number of indictments handed down to members of the bar. Bemoaning the magnitude of the situation, John Dean, counsel to the president, asked, "How in God's name could so many lawyers get involved in something like this?"[2] The acts of impropriety and unethical conduct these lawyers engaged in only served to further erode public confidence and respect for the legal profession. In the wake of Watergate, the HBA suffered an image crisis comparable to that of the era of the "shyster lawyer" at the turn of the century. Once again the HBA faced the challenge of restoring the "wonted honor" of the profession.

In a message to the membership in September 1973, HBA President Vincent W. Rehmet called on lawyers to rededicate themselves to participating in state and local bar associations and to represent clients "with the utmost fidelity, efficiency, and dispatch so as to deserve the respect we strive to command."[3] Houston lawyers heeded the call, and the following year President Ralph Carrigan sensed "a very strong increased awareness on the part of the many Harris County lawyers in the need to work as a unified Bar organization."[4]

While the Houston bar struggled to unify at the local level, Leon Jaworski traveled to Washington, D.C., to serve the nation as special prosecutor in the Watergate scandal. Jaworski's rigorous prosecution secured the release of the incriminating Nixon tapes and brought the prosecution to a successful conclusion. President Carrigan publicly thanked Jaworski for his role as special prosecutor, saying that Jaworski's "intelligence, dignity and quiet professionalism" was a "distinct service to the country" and to the legal profession.[5] Looking back on Watergate in 1981, Jaworski said that "Watergate, tragic as it was, demonstrated that American constitutionalism binds the strong and the powerful even as it embraces the weak and the oppressed."[6]

On the local level, the HBA instituted a series of special programs to restore public confidence in the legal profession. By the late 1970s and early 1980s, these programs helped to develop the HBA into a complex organization with the internal strength to implement a broad range of innovative services for the community.

The phenomenal growth of the association's continuing legal education programs (CLE) was an integral component of the HBA's efforts to raise professional standards.[7] Although many dedicated lawyers were behind the pioneering efforts of CLE, the primary advocate was Charlie Keilin, a man who consistently received the HBA's annual award for outstanding service because of his CLE accomplishments. Keilin's right-hand man was Firmin Hickey, Jr. Both Keilin and Hickey "were extremely enthusiastic and conscientious in working on CLE programs," and because of their efforts, Houston's CLE flourished.[8] Keilin did such a fine job pioneering the HBA's CLE programs that when Leroy Jeffers assumed the office of state bar president in 1973, Jeffers appointed Keilin chairman of the state bar Continuing Legal Education Committee. Jeffers attributed the "tremendous success of CLE in Texas in general and in Houston in particular . . . to the dedication and talents of Charles Keilin."[9]

The HBA started CLE in Texas. In the early years of CLE, lawyers came to Houston "from all over Texas because the State Bar didn't have these programs," recalls Justice Eugene A. Cook. "We had programs at the Rice Hotel where we would have 1,000 to 1,200 lawyers."[10] Some of the program topics were: Bar Economics, Medical Testimony in Personal Injury Litigation, Probate and Trust, Domestic Relations, Trial Practice and Procedure, Salvation for the Solo Practitioner and the Small Firm, and Strategy and Tactics in the Handling of Criminal Cases. Although the programs included speakers from around the country, the majority of experts came from Houston's own bar: Judge Ed Duggan, Sam Robertson, John J. Eikenburg, Charles W. Giraud, Eugene A. Cook, David Hittner, Ben L. Aderholt, Royce Till, James E. Brill, Joe Draughn, Jim Perdue, Bob Dunn, Tom Arnold, James A. Baker III, Joseph D. Jamail, Percy Foreman, and Richard "Racehorse" Haynes, to name just a few.

While CLE was coming into its own, the administration of Seaborn Eastland, Jr., began implementing the judicial evaluation poll recommended by the association directors in 1971. Don Fullenweider guided the Judicial Evaluation Committee through its infancy, and in July 1973 the HBA published the results of the first Texas judicial evaluation poll. "The early process of judicial evaluation was quite traumatic and created an unusual stir among the judges who perceived the evaluation program as a form of popularity contest," recalls James B. Sales. Despite the HBA's conviction that the program's "long-range potential in the field of judicial selection, tenure and compensation [was] unlimited," it was not until the 1980s that judicial evaluation became an accepted process of the bar association. "Now the results are eagerly awaited by the media as a means of assisting the electorate during elections," said Sales.[11] Although judicial evaluation remains controversial, the HBA leadership has consistently championed its value as a public service essential to the system of electing judges.

Until 1974, the HBA's unwritten tradition of rotating the position of president among the "big firms" remained unchallenged. That changed, however, when the firm of Bracewell & Patterson tried to steal the "big firm" spotlight. In 1974, Bracewell & Patterson offered one of its partners, Hal DeMoss, as a candidate for president even though it was Baker & Botts's turn to do so. According to journalist Griffin Smith, Jr.:

The contest became a colossal grudge match with both firms fighting for their self esteem. 'The activity at Baker & Botts was unbelievable,' recalls one young associate who lived through the experience there. 'Nobody seemed to be doing any work for a while—the associates certainly weren't. We were all on the phones, calling people to get out the vote. It was like saving Western Civilization.'[12]

In the end Baker & Botts succeeded in electing their candidate, Ralph Carrigan. Despite some hard feelings, Bracewell & Patterson joined the "Big Five" several years later and successfully ran their candidate, William Key Wilde, in 1982.[13]

Though challenged in 1974, the rotational system has stood the test of time and is accepted throughout the association as a fair way of giving both large and small firms an equal opportunity to set HBA policy. A potential problem with this "traditional system" is that it now takes about twelve years for a large firm to run a new candidate. As other firms grow in size and make contributions to the bar, the number of firms claiming "large firm" status could double, thus lengthening the time between candidates. As Pearson Grimes says, "it will be interesting to see if the large firms want to continue [the tradition] when they are delayed for twelve, fourteen, sixteen years in having a bar president. They may become disenchanted with the idea as well as some of the small firms and it will be interesting to see if that tradition continues."[14]

At the beginning of President Carrigan's term, the officers and directors of the HBA recognized that the activities of the association, although successful, were "extremely narrow in scope." The consensus was that the HBA had "a rather well-run operation serving [its] own members reasonably well," but that the association needed to expand its operation in the area of community service.[15] To accomplish this, the HBA instigated "Operation Reachout," a series of activities designed to bring the bar back into the community. Operation Reachout marked a significant change in the purpose of the HBA. Prior to this point in time, the HBA had focused primarily on what it could do for its own members. Although the HBA had always sought to do community service projects, they were not on the same scale as those of the late 1970s and 1980s. By the late 1970s the emphasis had shifted to what the HBA could do for the public.

There were essentially three reasons for this evolutionary change. The first was a significant increase in membership. In 1970, the HBA had approximately 2,500 members. By the late 1970s, that number had more than doubled to nearly 5,700. More members meant greater participation in bar projects. Coupled with the increase in manpower was a greater awareness among lawyers that they had a professional responsibility to serve the public and give something back to the community. Lastly, the HBA leadership realized that expanded service to the community was the bar's most effective public relations tool.

The first step in Operation Reachout was to establish a working relationship with the Harris County judiciary. According to HBA officers and directors, "Any lines of communication with any segment of the judiciary was tenuous to non-existent, relying almost in total upon individual personal friendships. In some instances even these lines had been strained by Texas' first judicial evaluation poll conducted two years earlier."[16] The HBA's solution to the problem of strained relations was the implementation of an informal luncheon series between lawyers and judges. Focusing initially on judicial problems and complaints, the luncheon discussions eventually addressed important substantive and procedural issues.

To better serve the public, the HBA initiated a fee arbitration committee, reorganized the Lawyer's Referral System, and expanded the traditional one-day observance of Law Day into a week-long program of events. More importantly, however, the association sponsored a news media seminar.

Since the late 1940s, the HBA had recognized the importance of public relations, but it was not until 1975 that the association forged a meaningful bond with the local news media. In January, a new Media Committee under the direction of Sherman Ross held a day-long seminar at the Rice Hotel for members of the Harris County news media. During the seminar, a panel of knowledgeable speakers covered a wide range of legal topics, which were designed to educate and assist the media in understanding the bar's daily work and problems in ensuring the efficient administration of justice in Harris County.[17]

Despite the successful programs of Operation Outreach, the HBA experienced a self-inflicted setback later in the year. A major issue in 1975 was whether Texans should accept or reject a new state constitution. To better educate its members and the public on such a vital issue, the HBA sponsored a special program for the Houston Bench and Bar, which featured four "very informed, dedicated men": Leroy Jeffers, Tom Stovall, Jr., Jim Vollers, and Clarence Guittard. Although each man "gave a masterful presentation of his views" and "tirelessly debated the issues," only a handful of the Houston Bar benefited because the vast majority did not attend. The poor showing prompted President George E. Pletcher to revise his October message in *The Houston Lawyer*. Initially intending to praise the bar for assuming an active leadership role, Pletcher instead criticized the bar for its indifference.

> You missed a lot, my fellow lawyers, and unfortunately, the loss is **not** limited—for had you been present, you could have gone forth well armed to legitimately argue your position to those who look to you for advice and leadership.
>
> Our Bar should feel acutely and keenly embarrassed! . . . Nothing short of a written apology to our distinguished guests will suffice. This is that apology. It is not enough![18]

As a service to its members, the HBA responded to the growing trend toward specialization by expanding its CLE programs and creating substantive law sections. In 1977, President Jack McConn had proposed that the HBA create substantive law sections; the following year his successor, Tom Arnold, pushed the proposal through. Arnold believed that the establishment of active substantive law sections within the association was his biggest contribution as president.[19]

In 1979, the HBA once again moved its offices. The increase in membership and an expanded administrative staff forced the HBA to seek larger office space in the Texas Commerce Bank Building at 707 Travis Street. When the HBA moved its offices to the Texas Commerce Building, the Inns of Court Club followed suit, locating itself on the fifteenth floor, where it remains to this day. In addition to overseeing the association's successful move into new headquarters,

President James Greenwood III emphasized the importance of developing a responsible and sensitive grievance system that was responsive to Houstonians who were "fed up" with lawyers.[20]

Early in his tenure as president, Charles R. (Bob) Dunn formed the Neighborhood Justice Center Committee and appointed the Honorable Frank G. Evans as its chairman. The committee's purpose was to "study and report on the feasibility of implementing an alternative dispute resolution system in the City of Houston."[21] Based on its study, the HBA created the Neighborhood Justice Center, Inc. (NJC), which quickly became "one of the best mediation programs in the nation." In 1985, the Neighborhood Justice Center changed its name to the Dispute Resolution Center and continued to expand the program to all areas of the city. The significance of the work begun by Judge Evans was that citizens were able to resolve minor disputes "without resorting to expensive legal action that would aggravate an already overcrowded court system."[22] Since 1980, the Dispute Resolution Centers' have assisted more than 60,000 citizens. Of those cases requiring mediation, more than 70% have resulted in an agreeable solution.[23]

In 1980, James B. Sales became president of the HBA. A firm believer in the axiom that "leadership is action and not merely a position or title," Sales sought to prepare the bar for the challenges of the new decade. A 1960 graduate of the University of Texas School of Law and a partner with the firm Fulbright & Jaworski, Sales was a man of both vision and vigor. He was the impetus behind the Houston *Pro Bono* Program and the Houston Bar Foundation—two projects that formed the nucleus of the HBA's community service programs.

Margaret Mirabal chaired the new committee on Legal Aid and *Pro Bono* Service, whose function was to identify those areas of legal practice where the public need for such services was not being met by existing agencies. As a result of Mirabal's "tireless and skillful leadership," the *Pro Bono* Committee formulated a viable *pro bono publico* program.[24] Initially called the Houston *Pro Bono* Program, the name was later changed to the Houston Volunteer Lawyers Program.

The HBA, Houston Lawyer Referral Service, and the Gulf Coast Legal Foundation jointly sponsored the Houston *Pro Bono* Program, which officially opened on May 18, 1981, to provide representation to the "working poor"—those individuals who made just enough money to disqualify them from receiving help from the Gulf Coast Legal Foundation, but who did not make enough to afford a lawyer. A $26,000 grant from the Legal Services Corporation and $60,000 in contributions from individual attorneys, law firms, and business enterprises funded the program during its first year of operation.[25] In that first year, more than 750 Houston attorneys participated in the program. According to Otway B. Denny, Jr., the *pro bono* program "function[ed] as a liaison between the client needing legal services and the volunteer attorney." The program received an average of eighty telephone calls a day.[26]

One of the most serious problems confronting the legal profession, in President Sales's opinion, was the issue of lawyer advertising. Prior to 1977, ethical rules of conduct essentially prohibited lawyer advertising. That changed in 1977, however, when the United States Supreme Court ruled in *Bates v. State Bar of Arizona* that the legal profession, acting through its bar association, could not use such rules of conduct to prohibit lawyer advertising.[27]

Despite its ruling, the Supreme Court specifically acknowledged that "reasonable restrictions on the time, place and manner of advertising" were permissible and that "we expect that the bar will have a special role to play in assuring that advertising by attorneys flows both freely and cleanly."[28] To conceptualize the HBA's "special role," Sales appointed David C. Redford to chair the new Committee on Lawyer Advertising. The committee had a twofold responsibility: to study the impact of advertising on the business and personal affairs of Houstonians as well as on the public image of the legal profession, and to formulate proposed voluntary guidelines for lawyer advertising that would "maintain the ethical standards of the profession and provide protection to the public."[29]

The thrust of the committee's guidelines was that an advertisement could contain factual information about the lawyers background, but that it should not contain sensational language nor predict future success. Sales believed that such "rational and reasonable advertising guidelines" were crucial because they "enabled the public to identify and locate qualified lawyers for particular legal problems without irresponsibly transforming lawyers into carnival hucksters and without further solidifying the negative attitude with which the public currently perceives the legal profession.''[30]

Due to the new problems confronting the legal profession as a whole, President Sales appointed the Long-Range Planning and Development Committee to "review all of the Bar Association's programs and to formulate appropriate objectives for the decade of the '80s."[31] Chaired by Terry O. Tottenham, the committee met monthly to review and discuss the work of each HBA committee and section. This marked the first time in the association's history that a standing committee was created specifically to examine the HBA's present operation and what the association should do to meet the challenges of the future. An organizational practice that enhanced the ability of the committee to make an impact was the appointment of the president-elect as chair of the Long-Range Planning Committee. This gives the president-elect an entire year to study the workings of the bar and to formulate an agenda before ascending the position of bar president.

One of the committee's recommendations was for the HBA to create a nonprofit charitable organization, much like the American Bar Foundation, so that the association could more effectively discharge its responsibilities both to the legal profession and to the community. Throughout the period 1981–82, President Joe L. Draughn's administration orchestrated a plan of action. The result was the Houston Bar Foundation (HBF). Characterized as "the charitable arm of the Houston Bar Association," the HBF provided grants for a variety of community service projects, to include: the Houston Volunteer Lawyers Project, the Neighborhood Justice Center, the Juvenile Justice Program, and the Appellate Judicial Study Project. As the foundation's first chairman, James B. Sales worked hard to solicit funds from law firms, foundations, corporations, and individuals. According to Sales, it took "shoe leather" and "knocking on doors" to obtain contributions for the upstart foundation.[32] The Rockwell Fund, Inc., made the first contribution to the HBF. Attorney Joe M. Green, Jr., president of the Rockwell Fund, Inc., continues to be a major supporter of the foundation. From an initial annual budget of $240,000, the HBF has grown into a $820,000 per year operation.

As mentioned, one of the programs funded by the HBF was the Houston Volunteer Lawyers Project (HVLP). As president, Albert B. Kimball, Jr., fought hard to keep the HVLP going. Given the social funding cutbacks of the Reagan administration, the HBA feared that the federal government might close down the Legal Services Corporation, whose local grantee was the Gulf Coast Legal Foundation. Kimball was concerned that an alternative legal services program was in place "to take over the flood of cases" should that shut down occur. Both President Kimball and Chairman Reggie Hirsch spent a great deal of time expanding and perfecting the HVLP.[33]

The HVLP became a great success because of the willingness of Houston lawyers to help others. The spirit of lawyer volunteerism is exemplified by the work of Scott J. Atlas. Characterized as "a tireless organizer of *pro bono* services," Atlas helped create the HVLP and was the sole architect of the Texas Appointments Plan, which provided counsel to indigent criminal defendants on appeal. As a result of his dedication and hard work, the American Bar Association honored Atlas in 1986 with its highest honor for an individual, the *Pro Bono Publico* Award.[34]

In 1981, Kay Sim became the new executive director of the HBA, a position she holds to this day. Sim began her work at the HBA in 1975 when she served as director of the Juvenile Justice Mock Trial Program, which exposed Harris County schoolchildren to the legal system. According to Sim, "This positive exposure to the legal system hopefully will deter the youth from entering the system as offenders."[35] In 1977, the Juvenile Justice Mock Trial Program won the State Bar of Texas' Certificate of Achievement, and the HBA honored Sim with the HBA Leadership Award for "outstanding work in the initiation and development of the Mock Trial Program in the public schools."[36] In James B. Sales's opinion, Kay Sim "has been the pivotal factor in the growth and prosperity of the Association."[37]

President Frank B. Davis also praised Sim for her hard work and dedication in running the association on a daily basis. Because of her many talents and exceptional staff members, there were few problems that interfered with Davis's agenda for 1984–85.[38] During his tenure, Davis emphasized lawyer professionalism and the importance of lawyer involvement in community affairs. "We all bemoan the fact that [lawyers] are not more highly regarded," said Davis. "I think you have to get out . . . in the community and show people that you are willing to try to do something to further the community effort, [regardless of] whether it helps you individually.''[39] Davis was also concerned about the need for change in judicial selection.

The election of Texas judges was a controversial issue throughout the 1980s. Many criticized a system that swept competent judges out of office simply because citizens cast straight party ballots. ''We have seen the spectacle of political sweeps, where landslides for a Republican or Democrat at the top of the ticket have senselessly swept out of office able and experienced judges who were nominees of the losing political party,'' said Ewing Werlein, Jr.[40] Member J. Edwin Smith criticized the HBA for failing to act on the issue ''whether from lethargy, timidity, or whatever.'' Smith pointed out that while the association did nothing for the past two years, the *Houston Chronicle* had ''seriously endeavored to alert this community to the need for a change.'' A staunch supporter of nonpartisan selection, Smith asked, ''What legitimate excuse can we as a bar association offer for abdicating our duty to the lawyers, the judiciary and the public?''[41]

President William Key Wilde agreed with Smith.

Today, Texas state judges are completely dependent upon success in partisan politics to survive in office. . . . We expect judges to be totally non-partisan in office, but we require them to be partisan politicians to obtain and hold their judicial offices. This paradox impairs the quality of our entire state judicial system.[42]

The partisan election of judges presents a twofold problem. First, judges must campaign to get elected, forcing them to solicit funds, which often come from the lawyers who practice before them. Not only is the appearance of impropriety an issue, but political campaigning is time-consuming. And second, partisan sweeps can ''oust experienced, fair judges and on occasion replace them with less qualified . . . judges.''[43]

Although the HBA has not lobbied for one particular method of selection, it has continued its judicial evaluation as ''an educational service for the voters'' in the hope of preventing straight-ticket voting.[44] Each election year the HBA conducts a poll of its members regarding the qualifications of candidates seeking judicial positions and releases the results to the news media. Ewing Werlein, Jr., believes that the HBA Judicial Preference Poll is a critical element in the battle to promote an independent judiciary. In the 1988 elections, Harris County voters followed the preferences of the HBA in twenty-five out of twenty-six races. Said Werlein:

> The evident public trend of following the lead of the HBA Preference Poll bodes well for an independent and high quality judiciary. It also imposes upon us a responsibility that must be taken very seriously. While it is certain that lawyers on the whole are better qualified to evaluate the qualifications of judicial candidates than are members of the general public, we too can make mistakes if we do not redouble our efforts carefully to evaluate on a nonpartisan basis the qualifications and attributes of those who seek election to the bench.[45]

Despite those who claim the polls are "a popularity contest" and that the results are "completely insignificant," the judicial evaluation poll is one of the citizen's best sources of information when it comes time to cast a vote.[46]

In October 1985, the HBA became the first local bar association in Texas to sponsor a "Town Hall" meeting. Concentrating on crime, housing, and social security issues that affected the elderly, the town meeting was designed to help the elderly with their unique legal problems. As an outgrowth of the meeting, the HBA initiated a new public service program called "Judicare" to provide free legal services to senior citizens over age sixty.

One HBA spokesman described Judicare as "the latest in a series of aggressive steps taken by the [HBA] to provide upgraded service to Houstonians who need legal help and also to improve the general public perception of lawyers."[47] The impetus behind the association's "aggressive steps" was President John J. Eikenburg. Eikenburg believed that he had a responsibility to improve the legal profession's public image. Operating under the theme "Lawyers Care," Eikenburg avoided the "flash-in-the-pan" public relations firm approach and emphasized community service projects "so that people really could have respect for lawyers."[48]

Judicare was a prime example of Eikenburg's internal public relations approach. Although the initial impetus behind Judicare was that it would improve the lawyer's image, it was the inherent value of the program that ultimately drove the HBA. Said Eikenburg:

> [Judicare] started out somewhat as a vehicle to improve our image, but as we got more and more into the details and discussion of the program, the genuine need became apparent. By the time we decided to implement Judicare, the emphasis and focus shifted to the merits of the program, how necessary and beneficial it was to the elderly, and away from what the program could do for the image of lawyers. In fact, that is more or less a by-product of the program.[49]

To serve a greater cross section of society, Eikenburg focused on implementing a free, monthly call-in program for Houstonians. In an interview with reporters, Eikenburg said, "There's a certain amount of legal information that people need to have just to walk around, and there was no place they could turn to ask simple legal questions. We're trying to meet that need." The result was "LegalLine," a project which grew out of the HBA's Law Day "Call a Lawyer" program. Frank Panzica, chairman of the LegalLine Committee, emphasized that LegalLine was "strictly a community service" and that lawyers were "not in this to get new business or make money." Any caller wishing to hire an attorney was told to contact the Lawyer Referral Service, Volunteer Lawyers Program, or other agency to be referred to an attorney.[50] The following year the LegalLine format was expanded to include free legal advice for Spanish-speaking Houstonians. The program was called "Consejos Legales" and represented "a unique cooperative effort between the HBA and the Mexican Bar Association in Houston."[51]

The success of LegalLine was a positive image booster for the HBA. In November 1986, *The Houston Post* saluted the "volunteer lawyers of the Houston Bar Association" for their work in the LegalLine program.[52] Bar members also used the media to defend the honor of the profession. John F. Rhem, Jr., countered public attacks with a lengthy article in the *Houston Chronicle* entitled "Who says lawyers don't care?" In his article, Rhem detailed how the HBA, the HYLA, and the Texas Accountants and Lawyers for the Arts provided free legal services to Houston artists and nonprofit arts organizations. The fact that three legal organizations were involved in the arts was "an indication of how lawyers care for their individual clients and their community," said Rhem.[53]

The Women's Auxiliary to the HBA also did its part to convey the image that "lawyers care." In 1983, the auxiliary began working on an annual award to honor Houston lawyers for their longtime community service. The auxiliary named the award the "Leon Jaworski Award" because Jaworski epitomized the qualities set forth in the criteria: "a member in good standing of the HBA who is civic-minded, professionally capable, socially and culturally concerned, family oriented, morally and spiritually aware."[54] Awarded in 1988, the first recipient was Thomas D. Anderson, a partner with the firm of Anderson, Brown, Orn & Jones. During his fifty-plus years of legal service, Anderson was also president of the Museum of Fine Arts and the Houston Grand Opera, as well as chairman of the Washington-on-the-Brazos State Park Association, the Bayou Bend Advisory Committee, and many other groups.[55]

Cognizant of its legal roots, the HBA celebrated Texas' sesquicentennial in 1986 by hosting a Texas Legal History Luncheon. Held at the Meridien Hotel, the HBA honored 176 of its members who had practiced law for fifty years or more. The HBA also exhibited historical legal documents, photographs, and artifacts from Texas and Harris County.[56] A group of Houston lawyers and judges celebrated the sesquicentennial by recreating the trial of a Texas hog farmer found guilty of larceny in 1836. The defendant, played by Michael Gallagher, was once again found guilty, but "was spared the punishment of thirty-nine lashes." The HBA and Harris County judges sponsored the event, which was held in the civil courthouse.[57]

The first Houston Law Week Fun Run was held on May 3, 1986. Sponsored by the Commonwealth Financial Group and coordinated by the Houston Bar Association and the Houston Young Lawyers Association, the event was open to the general public and all proceeds benefited the Center for the Retarded, Inc. In support of the event, Mayor Kathryn J. Whitmire proclaimed May 3, 1986, as Houston Law Week Fun Run Event Day. Since its inception, the Law Week Fun Run has been an annual success. *Human Powered Sports* magazine gave the 1988 Fun Run a 5+ rating out of a top rating of five, saying: "Now this is how every race in the Houston area should be conducted. Race organizers paying attention to details, large and small, made this event a smashing success."[58]

Throughout the 1980s the HBA continued to expand services in a variety of legal and social service areas. Given the increased cost of litigation and an overburdened judicial system, the growth and acceptance of "dispute resolution" as a valid forum for resolving differences was a significant legal development. To better educate Houston's lawyers in this growing area, President Harold Metts devoted an entire issue of *The Houston Lawyer* to Alternative Dispute Resolution. Metts credited Houston's "tremendous progress in this field" to the "overwhelming support and leadership provided by Chief Justice Frank G. Evans and other members of the Houston Bar Association."[59]

In the area of social services, President Raymond C. Kerr urged members in 1987 to support "Houston Lawyers for Hunger Relief," a program of the HYLA aimed at reducing hunger in Harris County. "Those of us who can, must help those who are less fortunate," said Kerr. The goal was for each lawyer to donate the fee or salary generated by one hour of legal service to the relief organization of his or her choice.[60]

The HBA was also one of the first local bar associations to tackle the challenge of illiteracy. President Kerr, a member of Mayor Kathryn Whitmire's Task Force on Literacy, believed that literacy was essential in a democratic society. "If a large number of the populace cannot comprehend the written word, they cannot participate in society."[61]

Another new service was the HBA's Amnesty Project, whose purpose was "to assist illegal aliens in attaining resident status in the United States." According to Kerr, there was "a stirring concern in the community that so-called legal advisors [were] taking advantage of [illegal aliens] by charging outrageous fees for their services." Once again, the HBA felt a responsibility to "stand up and address this need."[62] The culmination of that effort was the largest naturalization ceremony ever held in Texas. As part of its traditional Law Day activities, the HBA and the U.S. District Court for the Southern District of Texas sponsored a naturalization ceremony in which "more than 5,000 immigrants from 100 countries" took the oath of citizenship. The event was held in Hofheinz Pavilion on the University of Houston campus.[63]

When Ewing Werlein, Jr., took the gavel as president in 1988, he became the third member of his family to hold that honor. Ewing Werlein's great-uncle, Judge Presley K. Ewing, was president of the HBA in 1912. Judge Ewing was also the vice-president of the 1901 Harris County Bar Association, forerunner of the modern HBA. Werlein's father, Judge Ewing Werlein, served as president of the HBA in 1942.

The challenge to Ewing Werlein, Jr., was similar to the one faced by Judge Presley Ewing in 1901—to restore "the dignity of the profession." In 1988 the dignity was tarnished by a growing number of "Rambo" litigators—lawyers whose stock-in-trade was "discourteous, needlessly combative, rude and uncivil behavior."[64] To combat "Ramboism," Werlein appointed Director Charles "Reb" Gregg to chair a special committee on professionalism, whose mission was to propose guidelines for professional courtesy. The goal was "to set forth many of the generally unwritten principles which should guide us in representing zealously our clients while at the same time fulfilling our duties of respect to the judiciary and courtesy to opposing counsel," said Werlein.[65]

"Ramboism" was an outgrowth of the greed and cut-throat competition that characterized the 1980s. With more and more lawyers competing for clients and a greater emphasis on "billable hours," competition became ruthless. Corporations and clients also expected their lawyers to "win at all cost," thereby fostering an environment that contributed to a decline in civility. The emphasis on "the bottom line" left little time for experienced lawyers to develop a meaningful mentor relationship with beginning lawyers. Justice Eugene Cook says that he learned the practice of law under a mentor system that emphasized the training of young associates. "If you engaged . . . in the type of conduct we have today, you would have been fired immediately," says Justice Cook.[66] Raymond Kerr recalls the "gentleman's game" of the 1950s and 1960s "when most lawyers seemed to know each other, professional courtesy and camaraderie seemed significantly higher and as a result litigation flowed more smoothly."[67] Unfortunately, that spirit of collegiality deteriorated over time and forced the organized bar to take action.

Gregg's committee drafted a mandate based on the belief that "honesty, candor, and fairness" should characterize the conduct of lawyers. Amid "widespread criticism and declining public confidence in the legal system," the HBA directors unanimously adopted the mandate in April 1989. "The adoption of this mandate is intended to encourage and inspire all lawyers to follow the highest traditional standards of our profession," said Werlein.[68]

When Texas Supreme Court Justice Eugene A. Cook succeeded Werlein as president, Justice Cook "made it part of [his] crusade" to use all his power and influence to put a stop to Rambo lawyers. During his administration, Justice Cook had the mandate printed and distributed to every lawyer and judge in Harris County. To combat Ramboism at the state level, Justice Cook put together "The Texas Lawyer's Creed—A Mandate for Professionalism." Both the Supreme Court of Texas and the Court of Criminal Appeals adopted the creed, which was a milestone because it marked the first time a supreme court in the United States had ever adopted a statewide creed of professionalism.[69]

Despite the new mandate, unprofessional conduct has continued—even among HBA members. At a recent deposition involving two HBA lawyers, hostile verbal exchanges "escalated to fisticuffs" over a question of personal integrity. "Let's go out and have a fistfight, pal. When you start questioning my integrity, we're going to have a fistfight!" declared the offended attorney. Even though one of the clients tried to calm the two lawyers down, the dispute "escalated into a shoving match" and one of the attorneys allegedly threw a punch at the other. District Judge Dan Downey, himself an HBA member, found the attorneys' behavior so reprehensible that he ordered both to submit handwritten, 2,000-word essays on professionalism, and to perform community service in the form of free legal work. Said Judge Downey: "It's too bad because the vast majority of lawyers don't act like this, but when they do, it soils the entire profession. This little exchange won't disappoint the public at all. It really lives up to people's low expectation of lawyers, which is a shame."[70]

The vast majority of HBA members, however, adhere to the mandate. One HBA member, State District Judge Michael McSpadden, is waging a one-man battle to ban "disruptive behavior" from Harris County's criminal courts. "At a time when our legal profession is held with so little respect by the public, we have a responsibility to enforce strict standards of conduct which have been ignored by our courts for years," says Judge McSpadden.[71] It takes time for any profession to change its ethics, so although the Mandate on Professionalism has failed to eradicate all forms of Ramboism, former HBA president Pearson Grimes claims that the mandate has at least "[made] lawyers aware of their obligation as professionals."[72]

From its inception the HBA has had consistently dedicated leadership from its officers and board of directors. In keeping with that tradition, the presidents of the four years from 1988–1992 have made significant contributions in preparing the HBA for the 1990s. Ewing Werlein, Jr., and Justice Eugene A. Cook instigated and solidified the Mandate on Professionalism, thus combating and hopefully ending the trend of Rambo tactics which characterized the 1980s. Pearson Grimes and Ben L. Aderholt built on their predecessors' success and instigated innovative bar programs to serve both lawyers and the community. Grimes instigated the HBA's first coat drive for the homeless and emphasized *pro bono* legal services for Houstonians suffering from AIDS. Aderholt emphasized the role of lawyers in shaping the future of Houston's Central Business District and the importance of changing the partisan system of electing judges.[73] While vigorously supporting the bar's charitable efforts and its interaction with the public, Aderholt steered the association toward providing greater services to the lawyers themselves. For example, Aderholt designated April 1992 as "quality of life month" and created the Whole Life Study Committee to promote the development of skills for balancing professional career, personal, and family needs in order to improve the overall quality of life of association members. "We ought to examine what would make our professional life a healthy and balanced endeavor and to provide our membership with a few introspective moments along the way," says Aderholt.[74]

Like the HBA work that sought to restore public confidence in the wake of Watergate, the success of the new Mandate on Professionalism has paved the way for a resurgence in community service–oriented programs. The challenge to the HBA is to identify future legal trends and establish committees to meet those needs.

Epilogue

The HBA has a proud heritage of professional excellence and community service. The widely heralded community programs developed and implemented by the HBA to date attest to the vigorous and enthusiastic attitude of the association in fulfilling its responsibilities both to the legal profession and to the community at large. "One of the main reasons for the success of the Houston Bar Association is not any one individual," says Justice Eugene Cook. "It's because we have built on what those who have gone before us have done."[1]

Houston lawyers have continued the tradition of providing strong leadership outside the local bar as well. In 1988, the State Bar of Texas honored two outstanding members of Houston's judiciary: Judge Frank Evans and Judge David Hittner. Judge Evans received the President's Award for his tireless efforts "in making the Alternative Dispute Resolution process a reality in Texas." Judge Hittner received a Certificate of Merit for his work in the state bar's CLE program.[2] After serving as HBA president, James B. Sales served as the 108th president of the Texas Bar Association in 1988–89, and in 1991–92 Bob Dunn served as the state bar's 111th president.

As for HBA members who have served the public through political office, James Greenwood III has served with distinction on the Houston City Council. The honor for highest political achievement by an HBA member goes to James A. Baker III. A descendent of Captain

James Baker and for years a partner in the firm of Andrews & Kurth, James A. Baker III is the 61st Secretary of State.

As an institution, the HBA has approximately 9,900 members and new administrative offices in the First City Tower at 1001 Fannin that "fit the image of a dynamic, progressive leading bar association."[3] Of that 9,900, 75% are male and 25% are female. Although a woman has yet to serve as president of the HBA, in 1990 Melanie D. Bragg became the first woman to hold the office of president of the Houston Young Lawyers Association since the organization's founding in 1937.

Despite the association's "real effort" over the last twelve years to be more inclusive with Hispanics, African-Americans, and Asians, the representation of minorities in the HBA "is not as good as it should be," says former president Pearson Grimes. Grimes focused on this problem during his administration, but he says that it is difficult to attract racial minorities to the organized bar because they have "felt excluded for so long."[4] Justice Eugene Cook maintains that "involvement is a two-way street. If we're going to meld, to have a bar association where there is involvement from [minorities], then we're going to have to take the time to be interested in them."[5]

Another problem area is the rising cost of legal services. As an attorney for fifty-nine years, association member Roland B. Voight has observed major changes in the legal profession. "The volume of the law has ballooned and the attitude of many 'attorneys' has changed from placing emphasis on service to clients to emphasis on the fee," says Voight.[6] The profession still has been unable to shake the "emphasis on the fee" image that has tainted the profession in the eyes of the public. Pearson Grimes says that there is "a groundswell out there of public discontent with the high cost of legal services."[7] The challenge to the legal profession is to address that problem. To do so, however, will demand a new breed of lawyer. If the rising cost of overhead demands that lawyers charge increasingly higher fees, then is it even possible to provide legal services at a lower price? In the 1960s, change was brought about by the new breed of social lawyer. What kind of lawyer will emerge to solve this latest crisis?

Today the HBA is at a point where its community service projects are far beyond the bar's traditional role of ensuring equal justice. Projects like food drives, coat drives, Lawyers for Literacy, the

Campaign for the Homeless, and Special Olympics are more akin to pure philanthropy. This latest philanthropic spirit seems to be a result of the renewed concern over professionalism. Lawyers today are more concerned about community service than at any time in the history of the profession.

"A spirit of public service is an integral part or portion in the very definition of being a lawyer," says Justice Eugene Cook. "It means we care. It means that we're putting something back, that if there are those out there who need help, that we help them, that we spend and should spend a substantial portion of our time not just billing clients but providing services."[8]

To be effective, any organization committed to public service must establish goals, set standards, and pursue ideals—but realizing these objectives and holding onto them is a continuous struggle. Ideals like liberty, justice, and professionalism are attainable, if elusive, goals that a bar association can define and work toward. Unquestionably, there will always be unexpected challenges to achieving such goals, but if history is a guide to the future, the HBA has demonstrated that it has the leadership and dedication to confront new challenges and meet them head on.

Presidents of the Houston Bar Association, 1870–1993

James W. Lockett 1923
Hiram M. Garwood 1924
Richard T. Fleming 1925
W. L. Cook 1926
Ned B. Morris 1927
Frank Andrews 1928
Hugh F. Montgomery 1929
C. A. Teagle 1930
Capt. James A. Baker 1931
Lewis Fisher 1932
John H. Freeman 1933
W. P. Hamblen 1934
Calvin B. Garwood 1935
R. Wayne Lawler 1936
Albert J. Delange 1937
Judge Walter Montieth 1938
J. S. Bracewell 1939
W. J. Howard 1940
Murray G. Smyth 1941
Ewing Werlein 1942
Newton Gresham 1943
W. L. Kemper 1944
James L. Shepherd, Jr. 1945
Earl Cox 1946
Palmer Hutcheson 1947
Nowlin Randolph 1948
Leon Jaworski 1949
Herman Pressler 1950
T. Everton Kennerly 1951
Harry R. Jones 1952
Paul Strong 1953
Cecil N. Cook 1954
Lewis W. Cutrer 1955
Denman Moody 1956
William N. Bonner 1957–58

David T. Searls 1958–59
Joyce Cox 1959–60
Kraft W. Eidman 1960–61
Latimer Murfee 1961–62
Hall E. Timanus 1962–63
George T. Barrow 1963–64
Thomas M. Phillips 1964–65
W. James Kronzer 1965–66
Arthur P. Terrell 1966–67
Harry W. Patterson 1967–68
Leroy Jeffers 1968–69
W. Ervin James 1969–70
Royce R. Till 1970–71
Hartford H. Prewett 1971–72
Seaborn Eastland, Jr. 1972–73
Vincent W. Rehmet 1973–74
Ralph S. Carrigan 1974–75
George E. Pletcher 1975–76
John L. McConn 1976–77
Tom Arnold 1977–78
James Greenwood III 1978–79
Charles R. (Bob) Dunn 1979–80
James B. Sales 1980–81
Hon. Joe L. Draughn 1981–82
William Key Wilde 1982–83
Albert B. Kimball, Jr. 1983–84
Frank B. Davis 1984–85
John J. Eikenburg 1985–86
Harold Metts 1986–87
Raymond C. Kerr 1987–88
Ewing Werlein, Jr. 1988–89
Hon. Eugene A. Cook 1989–90
Pearson Grimes 1990–91
Ben L. Aderholt 1991–92
Otway B. Denny, Jr. 1992–93

Houston Bar Association Members Distinguished by Service to the State Bar of Texas and the American Bar Association

Norman G. Kittrell
1890–1891, President of the State Bar of Texas
Presley K. Ewing
1899–1900, President of the State Bar of Texas
Lewis R. Bryan
1902–1903, President of the State Bar of Texas
H. M. Garwood
1905–1906, President of the State Bar of Texas
Frank C. Jones
1916–1917, President of the State Bar of Texas
Claude Pollard
1920–1921, President of the State Bar of Texas
John C. Townes
1933–1934, President of the State Bar of Texas

David A. Simmons
  1937–1938, President of the State Bar of Texas
  1944–1945, President of the American Bar Association

James L. Shepherd, Jr.
  1946–1947, President of the State Bar of Texas
  1957–1958, Chairman of the ABA House of Delegates

Albert P. Jones
  1950–1951, President of the State Bar of Texas

Newton Gresham
  1956–1957, President of the State Bar of Texas

Leon Jaworski
  1962–1963, President of the State Bar of Texas
  1971–1972, President of the American Bar Association

Joyce Cox
  1964–1965, President of the State Bar of Texas
  1971–1974, Board of Governors of the American Bar
    Association

Thomas M. Phillips
  1967–1968, President of the State Bar of Texas

Leroy Jeffers, Sr.
  1973–1974, President of the State Bar of Texas

Gibson Gayle, Jr.
  1976–1977, President of the State Bar of Texas

Wayne Fisher
  1981–1982, President of the State Bar of Texas

Blake Tartt
  1983–1984, President of the State Bar of Texas

James B. Sales
  1988–1989, President of the State Bar of Texas

Charles R. (Bob) Dunn
  1991–1992, President of the State Bar of Texas

Houston Bar Association Historical Committee, 1986–1992

Chair:	Pearson Grimes	1986–87
	Kerry E. Notestine	1987–88
	Clinton F. Morse	1988–89
	Charles W. Giraud III	1989–91
	Jeffrey D. Dunn	1991–92
Vice Chair:	Rodney K. Caldwell	1991–92
Board Liaison:	Lester Hewitt	1988–89
	Joel Androphy	1989–90
	John F. Rhem, Jr.	1990–92
Members:	Hon. Sam Alfano	1991–92
	Mary E. Baker	1986–88
	Searcy Bracewell	1986–87
	James E. Brill	1989–91
	Rae Calvert	1988–89; 1990–92
	Hon. Mark Davidson	1989–92
	Juliette E. Daniels	1990–91
	Jeffrey D. Dunn	1986–92
	Michael P. Fleming	1989–91
	Roland Garcia	1991–92

Charles W. Giraud III 1989–92
Pearson Grimes 1986–88
Thomas W. Houghton 1991–92
Clinton F. Morse 1986–92
Anne Newtown 1989–92
Kerry E. Notestine 1986–92
Charlotte C. Orr 1988–91
William Pannill 1989–92
Jim Paulsen 1986–92
Joe Pratt 1986–89
R.L. Ragsdale 1987–88
James M. Riley, Jr. 1986–88
Paula Robertson 1991–92
Sheryl Roper 1986–87
James B. Rylander..................... 1991–92
Mark E. Steiner 1986–91
Hon. Thomas J. Stovall, Jr. 1988–92
Carlyle W. Urban 1987–88

HBA Staff Liaison: Kay Sim 1986–92

Notes

Introduction

1. Quoted in George M. Fuermann, "Notes and Documents: Houston, 1880–1910," *Southwestern Historical Quarterly* 71.2 (October 1967), p. 227.
2. Fuermann, p. 228.
3. For an informative account of the origins of the Houston Bar Association, see Mark E. Steiner, "'If We Don't Do Anything But Have An Annual Dinner': The Early History of the Houston Bar Association," *Houston Review* 11.2 (1989), pp. 95–110.
4. Steiner, p. 98; J. Willard Hurst, *The Growth of American Law: The Law Makers* (Boston, 1950), pp. 286–288; Lawrence M. Friedman, *A History of American Law*, 2nd ed. (New York: Simon and Schuster, 1985), pp. 648–650.
5. Steiner, p. 98; J. Gordon Hylton, "The Virginia Lawyer From Reconstruction to the Great Depression" (unpublished Ph.D. diss., Harvard University, 1986), pp. 4–6; Robert H. Wiebe, *The Search for Order, 1877–1920* (New York: Hill & Wang, 1967), pp. 111–132.
6. Kermit L. Hall, *The Magic Mirror: Law in American History*, (New York: Oxford University Press, 1989), p. 214.
7. Wayne K. Hobson, *The American Legal Profession and the Organizational Society, 1890–1930* (New York: Garland Publishing, 1986), p. 216.
8. Hall, p. 212.
9. Richard L. Abel, *American Lawyers* (New York: Oxford University Press, 1989), p. 45. According to Abel, the number of lawyers in the U.S. increased 63% between 1850 and 1870. Between 1870 and 1880, the number increased another 49% to a total of 60,626. (Table 22: Size of Profession and Population, 1850–1984.)

10. Justice Eugene A. Cook. Personal interview by Charles W. Giraud and Eric L. Fredrickson. December 14, 1990. HBA Archives. Justice Cook quotes Roscoe Pound's definition of a "profession," as it appears in Roscoe Pound, *The Lawyer from Antiquity to Modern Times* (St. Paul, Minn.: West Publishing Co., 1953), p. 5.

11. *The Houston Lawyer* 19.1 (August 1981), p. 4.

12. Thomas M. Phillips. Personal interview by Joe Pratt. May 27, 1988. HBA Archives.

13. Joe L. Draughn, "Bicentennial Prologue" to the 1976–77 HBA Membership Pictorial Roster.

Chapter One

1. Stephen F. Austin, letter to Josiah H. Bell dated March 17, 1829, Eugene C. Barker, ed., *The Austin Papers*, Vol. 2 (Washington, D.C.: U.S. Government Printing Office, 1928), p. 190.

2. Josiah H. Bell, letter to Stephen F. Austin dated March 13, 1829, *The Austin Papers*, Vol. 2, p. 182.

3. Stephen F. Austin, letter to Josiah H. Bell dated March 17, 1829, *The Austin Papers*, Vol. 2, p. 190.

4. In 1842 he superseded Isaac N. Moreland as chief justice of Harris County, and during his four-year term he adopted new rules of practice for the probate court; See Andrew Forest Muir, "Algernon P. Thompson," *Southwestern Historical Quarterly* 51.2 (October 1947), pp. 143–146.

5. The Allen Brothers purchased the land from Elizabeth E. Parrott, the widow of John Austin. See B. H. Carroll, *Standard History of Houston, Texas* (Knoxville: H. W. Crew, 1912), p. 26.

6. *Telegraph and Texas Register*, August 30, 1836, quoted in Carroll.

7. "An Act Locating Temporarily the Seat of Government," approved Dec. 15, 1836, 1st Cong., 1836 Republic of Texas Laws 1 H. Gammel, Laws of Texas 1138 (1898); "An Act Locating the Seat of Justice for the County of Harrisburg, and other purposes," approved Dec. 22, 1836, 1st Cong., 1836 Republic of Texas Laws 1 H. Gammel, Laws of Texas 1284 (1898). The first capitol of the Republic was a two-story frame building on the corner of Texas Avenue and Main Street, the present site of the Rice Hotel. A legislative act of December 28, 1839, designated the area that had been Harrisburg Municipality and Harrisburg County as Harris County in honor of pioneer John Richardson Harris; see Herbert Fletcher, ed., *Harris County: Republic of Texas, 1839–45* (Houston: Anson Jones Press, 1950), p. 7.

8. A. Pat Daniels, *Texas Avenue at Main Street: The Chronological Story of a City Block in Houston, The Most Significant Block in the History of Texas* (Houston: Allen Press, 1964), p. 3.

9. Daniels, p. 3.

10. Andrew Forest Muir, ed., *Texas in 1837: An Anonymous, Contemporary Narrative* (Austin: University of Texas Press, 1958), p. 166.

11. *Telegraph and Texas Register*, May 2, 1837.

12. *Telegraph and Texas Register*, May 26, 1837; *Telegraph and Texas Register*, September 30, 1837. See also William Fairfax Gray, *From Virginia to Texas, 1835, Diary of Col. Wm. F. Gray* (Houston, 1965), and Hugh Rice Kelly, "Peter Gray," *The Houston Lawyer* 13.1 (January 1976), p. 29.

13. *Telegraph and Texas Register*, June 3, 1837.

14. Maxwell Bloomfield, "The Texas Bar in the Nineteenth Century," *Vanderbilt Law Review* 32.1 (1979), pp. 269–271.

15. Gray, p. 226.

16. W. D. Wood, "Reminiscences of Texas and Texans Fifty Years Ago," *The Quarterly of the Texas State Historical Association* 5.2 (October 1901), p. 119.

17. Carroll, p. 115; Daffan Gilmer, "Early Courts and Lawyers of Texas," *Texas Law Review* 12 (June 1934), p. 450. John W. Moore was a signer of the Texas Declaration of Independence.

18. The first grand jury members were Benjamin Fort Smith, Edward Ray, Ben Stencil, Abraham Roberts, P. W. Rose, William Goodman, M. H. Bundic, William Burnett, John Goodman, Sr., Freeman Wilkerson, Gilbert Brooks, Thomas Hancock, Allen Vince, John Dunnan, John Earls, E. Henning, Andrew Long, and James House, Sr; Carroll, p. 36.

19. Bartholomew, p. 64; Mrs. Dilue Harris, "Reminiscences of Mrs. Dilue Harris," in *Houston: A Nation's Capital, 1837–1839*, edited by the Harris County Historical Society (Houston, D. Armstrong Co., 1985), p. 41.

20. Gilmer, p. 450.

21. Carroll, p. 37; For a scholarly treatment of Texas' early criminal law, see Charles S. Potts, "Early Criminal Law in Texas: From Civil Law to Common Law, to Code," *Texas Law Review* 21 (April 1943), pp. 394–406.

22. Andrew Forest Muir, "Augustus M. Tomkins, Frontier Prosecutor," *Southwestern Historical Quarterly* 54.3 (January 1951), p. 318.

23. As quoted in Muir, "Augustus M. Tomkins," p. 320.

24. Muir, "Augustus M. Tomkins," p. 321.

25. S. O. Young, *True Stories of Old Houston and Houstonians: Historical and Personal Sketches* (Galveston: Oscar Springer, 1913), p. 7.

26. Michol O'Connor and J. W. Johnson, "Harris County Courthouse: Some Historical Notes," *The Houston Lawyer* 12.0 (November 1975), p. 43.

27. Construction on the third courthouse began in 1860, but the Civil War interrupted its completion. During the war, the uncompleted structure was used as a cartridge factory and guardhouse for Union prisoners captured at Galveston and Sabine Pass; See O'Connor and Johnson, p. 44; S. O. Young, *A Thumb-Nail History of Houston, Texas* (Houston: Rein & Sons Co., 1912), pp. 53–54.

28. John H. Herndon, "A Diary of a Young Man," in *Houston: A Nation's Capital, 1837-1839*, edited by the Harris County Historical Society (Houston: D. Armstrong Co., 1985), p. 80.

29. Herndon, p. 85; Muir, "Augustus M. Tomkins," p. 318.

30. Herndon, p. 85.

31. Carroll, pp. 37-38; Herndon, p. 85; *Telegraph and Texas Register*, March 31, 1838. According to Carroll, Jones and Quick were "to be hung on the Friday following." Both Herndon and the *Telegraph*, however, state that the execution occurred on Wednesday.

32. Herndon, p. 86.

33. As quoted in Anthony Sheppard, "The Nineteenth Century Bench and Bar in Harris County, Texas," *The Houston Lawyer* 13.5 (July 1976), p. 14.

34. Wood, p. 119.

35. Mark E. Steiner, "'If We Don't Do Anything But Have An Annual Dinner': The Early History of the Houston Bar Association," *Houston Review* 11.2 (1989), p. 96.

36. Norman G. Kittrell, *Governors Who Have Been, and Other Public Men of Texas* (Houston, 1921), p. 185.

37. Kelly, p. 30; Kittrell, p. 185.

38. *Preface*, 40 Tex., pp. 7, 9, 11 (1874).

39. Kittrell, p. 185.

40. Kittrell, p. 185; *History of Texas with a Biographical History of the Cities of Houston and Galveston* (Chicago: Lewis Publishing Co., 1895), p. 600.

41. Gray & Botts was the forerunner of the Houston law firm of Baker & Botts. For the history of Baker & Botts, see Kenneth J. Lipartito and Joseph A. Pratt, *Baker & Botts in the Development of Modern Houston* (Austin: University of Texas Press, 1991).

42. David G. McComb, *Houston: The Bayou City* (Austin: University of Texas Press, 1969), p. 77.

Chapter Two

1. According to the Houston *Telegraph*, April 24, 1870, the Houston Bar Association organized on April 23, 1870; *ibid.*, November 24, 1870.

2. *Houston Telegraph*, August 22, 1868.

3. *Houston Telegraph*, February 2, 1870; *ibid.*, April 10, 1870; On Houston's crime and corruption during Reconstruction, see George M. Fuermann, "Notes and Documents: Houston, 1880-1910," *Southwestern Historical Quarterly* 71.2 (October 1967), pp. 227-228; *Big Town, Big Money: The Business of Houston* (Houston: Cordovan Press, 1973), p. 19.

4. S. O. Young, *True Stories of Old Houston and Houstonians: Historical and Personal Sketches* (Galveston: Oscar Springer, 1913), p. 14.

5. Marion Merseburger, "A Political History of Houston, Texas, During the Reconstruction Period as Recorded by the Press: 1868–1873," (Master's Thesis, Rice Institute, Houston, May 1950), p. 28.

6. Young, p. 14; See also *Big Town, Big Money: The Business of Houston*, p. 19.

7. For a detailed account, see Merseburger, pp. 48–49.

8. William S. Speer and John Henry Brown, eds., *The Encyclopedia of the New West* (Marshall, Texas, 1881), p. 192.

9. Maxwell Bloomfield, "The Texas Bar in the Nineteenth Century," *Vanderbilt Law Review* 32.1 (1979), p. 268.

10. *Houston Telegraph*, December 14, 17, 1869; *Houston Telegraph*, January 1, 4, 1870; *Houston Telegraph*, February 1, 1870.

11. For the number of lawyers, see *Houston City Directory* for 1870–71 (Houston: William Murray, 1870); Peter M. Rippe, "Other Landmarks of History," *The Houston Lawyer* (February 1976), p. 38; For lawyer office locations, see the *Houston City Directory* for 1897–98 and 1899.

12. B. H. Carroll, "The Bench and Bar," *Standard History of Houston, Texas* (Knoxville: H. W. Crew, 1912), p. 111.

13. For biographical information on Goldthwaite, see James D. Lynch, *The Bench and Bar of Texas* (St. Louis, 1885), pp. 503–504; For the details of the Goldthwaite plan, see Harold Platt, *City Building in the New South: The Growth of Public Services in Houston, Texas, 1830–1910* (Philadelphia: Temple University Press, 1983), pp. 27–28.

14. *Galveston Daily News*, October 4, 1874; *History of Texas, with a Biographical History of the Cities of Houston and Galveston* (Chicago, 1895), p. 601.

15. See the *Proceedings of the Texas Bar Association* for the years 1882, 1883, 1884, 1889. The firm name Gray & Botts changed to Gray, Botts & Baker in 1872 when Judge James A. Baker joined the partnership of Peter Gray and Walter Botts. When Peter Gray died in 1874, the firm name became Baker & Botts.

16. Kenneth J. Lipartito and Joseph A. Pratt, *Baker & Botts in the Development of Modern Houston* (Austin: University of Texas Press, 1991), p. 48.

17. Mary Lasswell, *John Henry Kirby: Prince of the Pines* (Austin: Encino Press, 1967), p. 56.

18. Lasswell, p. 75.

19. From *The Houston Post*, as quoted in Lasswell, p. 57. Quoted in Vera L. Dugas, "A Duel with Railroads: Houston vs. Galveston, 1866–1881," *East Texas Historical Journal* 2.2 (October 1964), p. 118.

20. Palmer Hutcheson, "Earliest Effort To Secure 25 Foot Channel Described," *Houston* 8 (November 1937), pp. 3–4.

21. Marilyn McAdams Sibley, *The Port of Houston: A History* (Austin: University of Texas Press, 1968), p. 135.

22. Quoted in Sibley, p. 136.

23. Colonel Thomas H. Ball, *The Port of Houston: How it Came to Pass* (Houston: reprinted from articles appearing in the *Houston Chronicle* and *The Houston Post*, August 2–November 1, 1936), pp. 21, 32.
24. Ball, p. 24.
25. *Proceedings Texas Bar Association, 1937*, p. 30.
26. Norman G. Kittrell, *Governors Who Have Been and Other Public Men of Texas* (Houston, 1921), p. 251.
27. Platt, p. 157.
28. Platt, p. 160.
29. Carroll, p. 115.
30. Figures are from the *Houston City Directory* for 1900–1901, and the *U.S. Bureau of the Census*.
31. O. M. Roberts, "Legal Education and Admission to the Bar," *Proceedings of the Third Annual Session of the Texas Bar Association* (1884), p. 47.
32. On bar admissions, see Ralph W. Yarborough, "A History of Law Licensing in Texas," *Centennial History of the Texas Bar* (1981), pp. 181–192; See also Stephen K. Huber and James E. Myers, "Admission to the Practice of Law in Texas: An Analytical History," *Houston Law Review* 15.3 (March 1978), pp. 485–533; Lasswell, p. 42.
33. Lasswell, p. 42.
34. "An act to amend title Ten chapter 2 of the Revised Civil Statutes," approved March 10, 1891, 22d Leg., 1891 Tex. Gen. Laws, ch. 22, at 23, 10 H. Gammel, *Laws of Texas* 25 (1898).
35. See the *Houston City Directory* for 1897–98 and 1899.
36. *The City of Houston, and Harris County, Texas. The World's Columbian Exposition Souvenir* (Houston: Post Engraving Company, 1893).
37. See Platt, pp. 132–133; *Houston Daily Post*, March 19, 1889.
38. *Houston Daily Post*, March 19, 1889.
39. *Houston Daily Post*, March 20, 1889.
40. *Houston Daily Post*, March 20 and 23, 1889.
41. Young, pp. 54, 154, 211, 154; See also Mark E. Steiner, "'If We Don't Do Anything But Have An Annual Dinner': The Early History of the Houston Bar Association," *Houston Review* 11.2 (1989), p. 97; *Houston City Directory, 1877–78*.
42. This account of Rice's death is based on three sources: Marie Phelps McAshan, *On the Corner of Main and Texas: A Houston Legacy* (Houston: Hutchins House, distributed by Gulf Publishing Co., 1985), pp. 121–128; Fredericka Meiners, *A History of Rice University: The Institute Years, 1907–1963* (Houston: Rice University Studies, 1982), pp. 11–14; Andrew Forest Muir, "Murder on Madison Avenue," in *William Marsh Rice and His Institute: A Biographical Study*, ed. Sylvia Stallings Morris (Houston: Rice University Studies, 1972), pp. 84–109.
43. McAshan, p. 124.
44. McAshan, p. 125.

45. According to Muir, Patrick had a languishing law practice in Houston, which was further hampered by allegations that he had obtained fees from both sides in a divorce case. Patrick further alienated the Houston legal community by moving for the impeachment of a federal judge in Galveston. When the judge instructed the district attorney to initiate disbarment proceedings against Patrick, Patrick decided it was time to leave Houston; see Muir, pp. 84–85.

46. McAshan, p. 127.

47. Muir, p. 102.

48. Meiners, p. 14.

49. *Houston Chronicle*, October 23, 1901; *Houston Chronicle*, November 1, 1901.

50. *Houston Daily Post*, July 30, 1901.

51. The details are from the *Houston Daily Post*, July 30, 1901.

52. *Houston Daily Post*, July 31, 1901.

53. *Houston Chronicle*, November 1, 1901; Kittrell, p. 239.

54. *Houston Chronicle*, October 25 and 26, 1901; See also Steiner, p. 100.

55. *Houston Chronicle*, November 7, 1901.

56. *The Houston Post*, November 10, 1901.

57. *Houston Chronicle*, December 2, 1901.

58. For biographical information on Brockman, see Ellis A. Davis and Edwin H. Grobe, eds., *The New Encyclopedia of Texas*, Vol. 2 (Dallas: Texas Development Bureau, 1925), pp. 1521–1522; *Houston Chronicle*, December 4, 1901.

59. *Houston Chronicle*, December 11 and 12, 1901.

60. *Houston Chronicle*, December 12, 1901.

61. *Houston Chronicle*, December 12, 1901; *Houston Daily Post*, December 12, 1901.

62. *Houston Chronicle*, December 14, 1901.

63. *Houston Daily Post*, December 13, 1901.

64. *The Houston Post*, December 15, 1901; Steiner, p. 103.

65. *Houston Chronicle*, December 23, 1901; Steiner, pp. 104–106.

66. Platt, p. 194.

67. Platt, pp. 182, 184.

68. *Houston Daily Post*, March 27, 1904.

69. *Houston Daily Post*, March 27, 1904; Steiner, p. 107.

70. Constitution and By-Laws of the HBA, 1904, Courtesy of the Houston Metropolitan Research Center (HMRC).

71. HBA Constitution and By-Laws, 1904.

72. Dinner program of the Fourth Annual Banquet of the Houston Bar Association, from the ''Houston Bar Association'' vertical file collection, HMRC.

73. *Houston Chronicle*, January 13, 1905.

74. *Houston Chronicle*, January 13, 1905; *Houston Daily Post*, March 14, 1905; For a detailed history of the Harris County Courthouse, see Michol O'Connor and J. W. Johnson, ''Harris County Courthouse: Some Historical Notes,''*The Houston Lawyer* 12.10 (November 1975), pp. 40–49.

75. O'Connor and Johnson, p. 48.

76. Ingham Roberts, "Evolution of Harris County Courthouse." Contained on p. 27 of the Ring Scrapbook at the HMRC.

77. Membership figures and operating budget are from the President's Report for 1910, HBA Archives.

Chapter Three

1. HBA President's Report for 1910, HBA Archives.

2. See "History of the Harris County Law Library," in the 1949 Catalog of the Harris County Law Library; *Texas Bar Journal* 1.4 (April 1938), p. 101; *New Encyclopedia of Texas* (Dallas: Texas Development Bureau, 1925), p. 1011.

3. For information on the changing role of bar associations, see Wayne K. Hobson, *The American Legal Profession and the Organizational Society, 1890–1930* (New York: Garland Publishing Company, 1986), pp. 262–313.

4. Joseph S. Auerbach, *The Bar of Other Days* (New York: Harper & Brothers, 1940), p. 7.

5. Kermit L. Hall, *The Magic Mirror: Law in American History* (New York: Oxford University Press, 1989), p. 212.

6. Wayne K. Hobson, "Symbol of the New Profession: Emergence of the Large Law Firm, 1870–1915," in *The New High Priests: Lawyers in Post-Civil War America*, Gerald W. Gawalt, ed.(Westport: Greenwood Press, 1984), p. 9.

7. Unidentified newspaper article in the Mayor Ben S. Campbell Collection, MSS 283, Box 2, Houston Metropolitan Research Center.

8. *Houston Chronicle*, January 7, 1912.

9. *Houston Chronicle*, January 8, 1913.

10. Colonel Thomas H. Ball, *The Port of Houston: How it Came to Pass* (Houston: reprinted from articles appearing in the *Houston Chronicle* and *Post*, August 2–November 1, 1936), p. 43.

11. *The Houston Post*, March 20, 1942.

12. The description of the 1914 campaign is based on Sean Collins Murray, "Texas Prohibition Politics, 1887–1914" (Masters Thesis, University of Houston, Houston, Texas, 1968), pp. 107–121; Ball, p. 129.

13. *Proceedings of the Thirty-sixth Annual Session of the Texas Bar Association* (1917), p. 78.

14. *Proceedings of the Thirty-sixth Annual Session of the Texas Bar Association* (1917), p. 81.

15. *Proceedings of the Thirty-sixth Annual Session of the Texas Bar Association* (1917), pp. 5–7.

16. See David G. McComb, *Houston: The Bayou City* (Austin: University of Texas Press, 1969), p. 163; *The Houston Post*, August 25, 1917. For the definitive account of the Houston Riot, see Robert V. Haynes, *A Night of Violence: the Houston Riot of 1917* (Baton Rouge: Louisiana State University Press, 1976).

17. Haynes, p. 196.
18. Haynes, p. 195.
19. *Houston Daily Post*, August 25, 1917; Haynes, p. 198.
20. Haynes, p. 206.
21. *Houston* (August 1944), p. 18.
22. For biographical information on Garwood, see *New Encyclopedia of Texas*, p. 1323; Resolution of the Houston Bar Association in Memory of Calvin Baxter Garwood, HBA Archives.
23. Mrs. W. M. Baines, ed. *Houston's Part in the World War* (Houston, 1919), p. 25; The Harris County Bar Association paid tribute to Captain Burkett with a special plaque dedicated to "A gallant knight without fear and without reproach." The plaque is currently in the possession of Harris County.
24. For the names of each chairman, see the division rosters of the Houston War Savings Committee as contained in the "Houston—World War I" vertical file folder at the Houston Metropolitan Research Center; In 1905 Cole founded the law firm which is today Patterson, Boyd, Lowery & Aderholt. For information on Cole see *New Encylopedia of Texas*, p. 1362; *History of the Law Firm of Patterson, Boyd, Lowery & Aderholt.*
25. *Proceedings Texas Bar Association,* Vol. 52 (1933), p. 91.
26. Walter L. Buenger and Joseph A. Pratt, *But Also Good Business: Texas Commerce Banks and the Financing of Houston and Texas, 1886–1986* (College Station: Texas A & M University Press, 1986), pp. 64, 81.
27. Kenneth J. Lipartito and Joseph A. Pratt, *Baker & Botts in the Development of Modern Houston* (Austin: University of Texas Press, 1991), p. 109.
28. As quoted in Griffin Smith, Jr., "Empires of Paper," *Texas Monthly* 1.10 (November 1973), p. 57.
29. Charles C. Alexander, *The Ku Klux Klan in the Southwest* (Lexington: University of Kentucky Press, 1965), p. 13; On the Klan in Texas see also Charles C. Alexander, "Crusade for Conformity: The Ku Klux Klan in Texas, 1920–1930," *Texas Gulf Coast Historical Association* 6.1 (August 1962); Don E. Carleton, *Red Scare! Right-wing Hysteria, Fifties Fanaticism, and their Legacy in Texas* (Austin: Texas Monthly Press, 1985), p. 8; *Houston: A History and Guide* (Houston: The Anson Jones Press, 1942), p. 115; For an informative account of the Klan in Houston, see Casey Greene, "Guardians Against Change: The Ku Klux Klan in Houston and Harris County, 1920-1925," *Houston Review* 10.1 (1988), pp. 3–20.
30. Greene, p. 9; *Houston Chronicle*, January 14, 1923.
31. Alexander, *The Ku Klux Klan in the Southwest*, p. 41; *Houston Chronicle*, February 6, 1921; Greene, p. 9.
32. *Houston Chronicle*, August 26, 1921; Greene, p. 11.
33. As Quoted in Greene, p. 11.
34. *The Houston Post*, June 21 and 29, 1923.
35. Greene, pp. 16–18.
36. Alexander, *The Ku Klux Klan in the Southwest*, p. vii.

37. HBA Minutes, January 8, 1924.

38. HBA Minutes, January 8, 1924.

39. U.S. Bureau of the Census, *Seventeenth Census of the United States: 1950* (Washington, D.C., 1950), Table 43–11.

40. Reginald Heber Smith. *Justice and the Poor* (New York: Carnegie Foundation, 1919), Table I.

41. *Houston City Directory, 1925* (Houston: R. L. Polk & Co., 1925).

42. Norman H. Beard, ed. *The Municipal Book of the City of Houston, 1922* (Houston, Texas: 1922), p. 37. Courtesy of Special Collections, University of Houston.

43. HBA Minutes, February, 1924. HBA Archives.

44. Ben C. Connally. Personal interview by Louis Marchiafava. April 2, 1975. Courtesy of HMRC. Oral History Collection #30.

45. *Bar Association Syllabus*, June 22, 1925, p. 5.

46. *Bar Association Syllabus*, September 19, 1925, p. 1.

47. HBA Minutes, September 24, 1925.

48. HBA Minutes, December 30, 1926; HBA Minutes, January 1928.

49. HBA Minutes, December 31, 1929.

50. Letter to George A. Hill, Jr., from the Voluntary Committee of Lawyers, Inc., June 30, 1930. George A. Hill, Jr., collection. HMRC.

51. *Houston Press*, September 27, 1927.

52. HBA letter, April 26, 1929. George A. Hill, Jr., collection.

53. *Houston Bar Journal* 1.1 (November 1930), p. 1.

54. George A. Butler. Personal Interview by Thomas H. Kreneck and Louis Marchiafava. November 18, 1982. HMRC.

55. Searcy Bracewell, *Bracewell & Patterson: "Some Early Recollections,"* (unpublished paper, Bracewell & Patterson, Houston 1981), p. 4. (Courtesy of Bracewell & Patterson.)

56. For information on Baker, see Jesse Andrews, "A Texas Portrait: Capt. James A. Baker, 1857–1941," *Texas Bar Journal* 24.2 (February 1961), pp. 110–11, 187–89.

57. McComb, p. 170.

58. Letter from Sam Streetman to Jesse H. Jones, June 25, 1932. Andrews & Kurth Historical Archives.

59. *Houston* (August 1933), p. 3.

60. For information on the "8F Crowd," see Chandler Davidson, "Houston: The City Where the Business of Government is Business," in Wendall Bedichek and Neal Tannhill, eds., *Public Policy in Texas* (New York: Scott Foresman, 1982), p. 278; Joe R. Feagin, *Free Enterprise City: Houston in Political-Economic Perspective* (London: Rutgers University Press, 1988), pp. 107–108, 124–136.

61. HBA Minutes, October 29, 1936.

62. HBA Minutes, February 16, 1937; For a detailed history of the Houston Law School, see Michael R. Davis, "A History of the Houston Law School," *The Houston Lawyer* 15.2 (Summer 1978), pp. 26–41 and *The Houston Lawyer* 16.1 (Fall 1978), pp. 30–38.

63. Report of the Committee on Legal Education and Admission to the Bar, "Legal Education and Admission to the Bar," *Texas Bar Journal* 1.7 (July 1938), pp. 196–199.

64. Robert L. Cole, Jr., responses to the HBA's History Questionnaire, 1986. HBA Archives.

65. Information on the Junior Bar is taken from David C. Redford, "The Houston Junior Bar Association: Its Past, Present and Future," *The Houston Lawyer* (December 1970), pp. 7–21. The Houston Junior Bar Association was later renamed the Houston Young Lawyers Association (HYLA).

66. Arthur P. Terrell. Personal Interview by Pearson Grimes. HBA Archives.

67. *Houston Bar Journal* 1.1 (November 1930), p. 6.

68. The averages are based on the age of each president at the time he held office, which was calculated based on each man's date of birth as it appears in such contemporary works as *Men of Texas, Standard Blue Book of Houston, The New Encyclopedia of Texas*, as well as memorials passed by the Houston and Texas Bar associations.

69. For biographical information on Simmons see the *Houston Biography Scrapbook, Men*, Vol. 16, HMRC.

70. HBA Minutes, November 9, 1937.

71. HBA Minutes, February 26, 1938.

72. The *Syllabus* 2.1 (April 1938).

73. The *Syllabus* 2.1 (April 1938); *Texas Bar Journal* 1.5 (May 1938), p. 125.

74. *Houston Press*, April 5, 1938, from the Houston Legal Aid vertical file collection of the HMRC.

75. *Houston Bar Journal* 1.7 (May 1931), p. 1.

76. HBA Minutes, October 20, 1938.

77. HBA Minutes, January 7, 1939.

78. Bracewell, pp. 3, 10. (Courtesy of Bracewell & Patterson).

79. *Texas Bar Journal* 2.3 (March 1939), p. 86.

80. HBA Minutes, September 27, 1939.

81. *Texas Bar Journal* 3.1 (January 1940), p. 15.

82. Fred Parks. Personal interview by Eric L. Fredrickson. June 19, 1990. HBA Archives; The description of Ruth Laws's duties is from the *Texas Bar Journal* 3.1 (January 1940), pp. 15–16.

83. Fred Parks interview.

84. Fred Parks interview.

85. The name of the first Texas woman lawyer was Hortense Ward; For an excellent study on women lawyers, see Karen Berger Morello, *The Invisible Bar: The Woman Lawyer in America 1638 to the Present* (Boston: Beacon

Press, 1986); For the general impressions of four Houston women, see Judge Geraldine B. Tennant, Doris E. Anderson, Mildred H. Rouse, and Barbara Finney. Personal interviews by Eric L. Fredrickson. March 30, 1990. HBA Archives.

86. Barbara Finney interview.

87. Quote is by Ms. Dorothy C. Most and is taken from the *Houston Biography Scrapbook of Women*, Vol. 17c, HMRC.

88. Billye N. Russell, responses to the HBA's History Questionnaire, 1986. HBA Archives.

89. Russell questionnaire; Joyce Burg. Personal interview by Eric L. Fredrickson. October 1, 1990. HBA Archives.

90. HBA Minutes, June 13, 1939.

91. *Texas Bar Journal* 2.3 (March 1939), p. 86.

92. Durell M. Carothers, responses to the HBA's History Questionnaire, 1986. HBA Archives.

93. *Texas Bar Journal* 2.3 (March 1939), p. 85.

94. *Texas Bar Journal* 3.4 (April 1940), p. 162.

95. Redford, p. 9.

96. *Houston* (February 1941), p. 33.

97. Fred Parks interview.

Chapter Four

1. *Houston Bar Bulletin* (December 1941).

2. See *Baker, Botts in World War II: A Collection of Narrative Accounts of their Service Experiences*, written by men of the law firm of Baker, Botts, Andrews & Wharton, Houston, Texas (North River Press, 1947); For a complete list of those HBA members who served in World War II, see the HBA's "Roll of Honor" plaque, which contains the names of 156 members "who have answered the call to the colors." The plaque is currently in the possession of Harris County.

3. HBA Minutes, June 15, 1942.

4. Denman Moody, "War History," in *Baker, Botts in World War II: A Collection of Narrative Accounts of their Service Experiences*, p. 517.

5. For Jaworski's role in the war crime trials, see his memoir, Leon Jaworski, *After Fifteen Years* (Houston: Gulf Publishing, 1961); Leon Jaworski with Mickey Herskowitz, *Confession and Avoidance: A Memoir* (Garden City, New York: Anchor Press/Doubleday, 1979), p. 102.

6. Jaworski with Herskowitz, p. 103.

7. Jaworski with Herskowitz, p. 107.

8. Jaworski with Herskowitz, p. 117.

9. *Houston Bar Bulletin* (January 1943).

10. W. Carroll Barnett, Jr., responses to the HBA's History Questionnaire, 1986. HBA Archives.

11. Fred Parks. Personal interview by Eric L. Fredrickson. June 19, 1990. HBA Archives.

12. *The Houston Lawyer*, Centennial Issue 8.6 (June 1971), p. 11.

13. HBA Minutes, August 4, 1943.

14. HBA Report of the President, 1945.

15. HBA Report of the President, 1945, HBA Archives; HBA Minutes, March 3, 1944.

16. Dillon Anderson, "My Own Version of My Service in the Army in World War II," in *Baker, Botts in World War II: A Collection of Narrative Accounts of their Service Experiences*, p. 54.

17. *The Houston Post*, August 4, 1986.

18. Searcy Bracewell, *Bracewell & Patterson: "Some Early Recollections,"* (unpublished paper, Bracewell & Patterson, Houston 1981), p. 4. (Courtesy of Bracewell & Patterson.)

19. Bracewell, p. 14.

20. George A. Butler. Personal Interview by Thomas H. Kreneck and Louis Marchiafava. November 18, 1982. HMRC.

21. For a good overview of the impact of World War II on legal-aid work, see Reginald Heber Smith, "Legal Aid During the War and After," *American Bar Association Journal* 31 (January 1945), pp. 18–21.

22. *Houston Bar Bulletin* (April 1944).

23. *Houston Bar Bulletin* (June–July 1945).

24. HBA President's Report for 1945, p. 6. HBA Archives.

25. American Bar Association Annual Report, 1945 by David A. Simmons. Contained in the G. H. Hill, Jr., Collection, MSS 71, Box 15. Courtesy of the HMRC.

26. The figures are from the "Report of the Standing Committee on Legal Aid Work," *Annual Report of the American Bar Association* 75 (Chicago: ABA, 1950), p. 472.

27. HBA Minutes, August 19, 1948.

28. *The Houston Post*, December 12, 1948.

29. *Houston Bar Bulletin* (October 1948).

30. *The Houston Post*, December 12, 1948.

31. For additional information on Cullen's donation, see *The Houston Lawyer* 2.4 (February 1965), p. 4. See also the *Houston Press*, January 10, 1950. Courtesy of HMRC, RG D5, *Houston Press* Collection.

32. *The Houston Lawyer* 2.4 (February, 1965), p. 4.

33. HBA Report of the President, 1949.

34. HBA Minutes, March 26, 1948; HBA Minutes, June 1, 1949; *Houston Bar Bulletin* (June–July 1949); HBA Report of the President, 1949.

35. All figures are from the HBA Report of the President for 1950 and 1952. HBA Archives.

36. *The Houston Lawyer* (February 1965), p. 5.

37. For a description of the "Plan" see Cecil E. Burney, "Texas Bar Acts on Legal Aid: 'Equal Justice Under Law'" *American Bar Association Journal* 38 (May 1952), pp. 396–397.

38. The information on Birmingham and New Orleans is from Frances Craighead Dwyer, "The Development of the Legal Aid Movement in the Southeast," *Tennessee Law Review* 22 (1951–53), pp. 497–501.

39. *Houston Bar Bulletin* (May 1947). The 1950 U.S. Census indicates that Houston had thirty women who were either lawyers or judges; *U.S. Census of Population: 1950*, Vol. II, Part 43, Chapter C, Table 78 (Washington, D.C.: U.S. Government Printing Office, 1950).

40. Information on the Women's Auxiliary is from "The History of the Women's Auxiliary to the Houston Bar Association," which appears in the auxiliary's 1986–1987 yearbook.

41. *Houston Bar Bulletin* (December 1950).

42. HBA Minutes, April 19, 1946; HBA Minutes, May 10, 1946.

43. HBA Report of the President, 1950. HBA Archives.

44. HBA Report of the President, 1950. HBA Archives.

45. HBA Report of the President, 1950. HBA Archives.

46. HBA Minutes, October 30, 1950.

47. For a scholarly treatment of Houston's Red Scare, see Don E. Carleton, *Red Scare! Right-wing Hysteria, Fifties Fanaticism, and Their Legacy in Texas* (Austin: Texas Monthly Press, 1985).

48. *The Houston Post*, August 31, 1953.

49. See *Application of Levy*, 214 F.2d 331 (5th Cir. 1954), *rev'd per curiam*, 348 U.S. 978 (1955); Leroy Denman Moody, Tom M. Davis, and Frank J. Knapp represented the HBA.

50. T. Everton Kennerly. Personal interview by Kerry Notestine. August 1987. HBA Archives.

51. *Houston Law Review* 6.5 (May 1969), p. 1017.

52. T. Everton Kennerly interview.

53. HBA Report of the President, 1951.

54. Quoted in the *Houston Chronicle*, October 14, 1952.

55. HBA Report of the President, 1950; T. Everton Kennerly interview.

56. *The Houston Post*, June 18, 1953.

57. *Houston Press*, February 13, 1953. "Judge" Roy Hofheinz served as Houston's mayor from 1953–1954. A colorful personality in Houston's history, Hofheinz is best remembered as builder of the Houston Astrodome. His son, Fred Hofheinz, served as Houston's mayor from 1974–1978.

58. Carleton, pp. 12, 135–136.

59. Carleton, pp. 162, 164.

60. As quoted in Carleton, p. 212.
61. As quoted in Carleton, p. 214.
62. Carleton, p. 228.
63. Clinton F. Morse. Personal letter to author. November 21, 1990.
64. Jim D. Bowner, "The Presidents" in the *Centennial History of the Texas Bar, 1882–1982*, by the Committee on History and Tradition of the State Bar of Texas (Burnet, Texas: Eakin Press, 1981), p. 107.
65. Bowner, p. 117.
66. For more information on Cutrer's political background see Leah Brooke Tucker, "The First Administration of Mayor Lewis Cutrer of Houston, 1958–1960," *East Texas Historical Journal* 12.1 (Spring 1974), p. 39.
67. Tucker, p. 41.
68. Tucker, p. 42.
69. For more information on Cutrer's role see Tucker, pp. 42–43.
70. *Houston Bar Bulletin* (May 1958), p. 3.
71. *Houston Bar Bulletin* (September 1959), p. 4.
72. *Houston Bar Bulletin* (October 1959), p. 1.
73. *Houston Bar Bulletin* (November 1959), p. 3.
74. *Houston Bar Bulletin* (November 1959), p. 3.
75. *Houston Bar Bulletin* (February 1969), p. 1.
76. *Houston Bar Bulletin* (April 1960), p. 1.
77. W. James Kronzer. Personal interview by Clinton F. Morse and Eric L. Fredrickson. June 26, 1990. HBA Archives.
78. *Houston Bar Bulletin* (June 1960), p. 1.

Chapter Five

1. Constitution and By-Laws of the Houston Bar Association, 1951; *Houston Bar Bulletin* (August 1960).
2. *Houston Bar Bulletin* (February 1960), p. 1.
3. HBA Minutes, December 27, 1962.
4. Hall E. Timanus. Personal statement. HBA Archives.
5. Polk's *Houston City Directory, 1960* lists 10 companies under photocopying and photoprinting in the Yellow Pages. L. L. Ridgway, Inc., offered such services but was not listed in the Yellow Pages under those categories.
6. Clinton F. Morse during W. James Kronzer interview. Personal interview by Clinton F. Morse and Eric L. Fredrickson. June 26, 1990. HBA Archives.
7. Hartford H. Prewett. Personal interview by James M. Riley, Jr. HBA Archives.
8. Judge Carl Walker, Jr. Personal interview by Eric L. Fredrickson, July 24, 1990. HBA Archives.
9. Judge Carl Walker, Jr., interview.

10. George T. Barrow. Personal interview. HBA Archives.

11. W. James Kronzer. Personal interview by Clinton F. Morse and Eric L. Fredrickson. June 26, 1990. HBA archives.

12. *Houston Chronicle*, September 1, 1965.

13. Judge Carl Walker, Jr., interview.

14. George T. Barrow interview.

15. George T. Barrow interview.

16. Transcript of Proceedings of General Membership Meeting of the Houston Bar Association, May 8, 1964; *The Houston Lawyer*, Centennial Issue 8.6 (June 1971), pp. 13–14.

17. *The Houston Lawyer* 4.5 (March 1967).

18. Civil Statutes of the State of Texas, Articles 1917 and 1958.

19. *Gideon v. Wainwright*, 372 U.S. 335 (1963).

20. Transcript of Proceedings of General Membership Meeting of the Houston Bar Association, May 8, 1964.

21. Thomas M. Phillips, "The Houston Plan: An Overview," *Texas Bar Journal* 29.9 (October 1966), p. 819.

22. Funding for the criminal defender program is covered in the *The Houston Post*, May 1, 1966, Sec. 3, p. 16. The civil branch is covered in the *Houston Chronicle*, April 26, 1966.

23. *The Houston Post*, March 13, 1966.

24. Thomas M. Phillips. Personal interview by Joe Pratt. May 27, 1988. HBA Archives.

25. *The Houston Lawyer* 2.12 (October 1965), p. 6.

26. Thomas M. Phillips interview.

27. W. James Kronzer interview.

28. J. Jackson Eaton, "External Factors which affect the HLF's Organization and Operations," in Daniel L. Rotenberg, "The HLF as a Failure," in Rotenberg, Daniel L., ed. "Legal Services for the Poor—Houston: An Analysis of the Houston Legal Foundation, An OEO Funded Legal Services Program," *Houston Law Review* 6.5 (May 1969), p. 1004.

29. Eaton, p. 1005.

30. Eaton, p. 1005.

31. Mark B. Raven, "HLF Value Goals and Internal Operations," in Rotenberg, p. 1052.

32. *The Houston Post*, September 13, 1966.

33. See *Touchy v. Houston Legal Foundation*, 417 S.W.2d 625 (Tex. Civ. App.— Waco 1967), *rev'd*, 432 S.W.2d 690 (Tex. 1968).

34. Quoted in the *The Houston Lawyer* 4.6 (March 1967), p. 13.

35. *The Houston Lawyer* 4.5 (March 1967), p. 14.

36. *Touchy v. Houston Legal Foundation*, 432 S.W.2d 690, 694 (Tex. 1968).

37. *Scruggs v. Houston Legal Foundation*, 475 S.W.2d 604 (Tex. Civ. App.— Houston [1st Dist.] 1972, no writ).

38. Rotenberg, *Houston Law Review* 6.5 (May 1969), p. 1224.
39. Raven, p. 1062.
40. Raven, p. 1062.
41. *The New York Times*, September 20, 1966, p. 32, col. 3.
42. Rotenberg, p. 1224.
43. Jeron L. Stevens, "The HLF as a Success," in Rotenberg, p. 1220.
44. Stevens, p. 1221.
45. Thomas M. Phillips interview.
46. News clipping contained in the "1960's HBA Scrapbook." HBA Archives.
47. Searcy Bracewell, *Bracewell & Patterson: "Some Early Recollections,"* (unpublished paper, Bracewell & Patterson, Houston 1981), p. 13. (Courtesy of Bracewell & Patterson.)
48. Clinton F. Morse. Personal interview by Eric L. Fredrickson. June 26, 1990. HBA Archives.
49. From the pamphlet "Recommended Minimum Fee Schedule of the Houston Bar Association" 1966.
50. From the pamphlet "Recommended Minimum Fee Schedule of the Houston Bar Association" 1966.
51. From the pamphlet "Recommended Minimum Fee Schedule of the Houston Bar Association" 1966.
52. Arthur P. Terrell, responses to the HBA's History Questionnaire, 1986. HBA Archives.
53. *Houston Chronicle*, Texas Magazine Section, September 22, 1968.
54. *The Houston Post*, January 25, 1966.
55. *The Houston Lawyer* 4.6 (April 1967), p. 12.
56. *The Houston Post*, January 25, 1966.
57. *The Houston Lawyer* 4.9 (July 1967), pp. 4–5.
58. Earlier in 1968 a group of lawyers had founded the Inns of Court Club as a social vehicle for lawyers. Every Friday, members of the HBA met for lunch and refreshments in a room at the Houston Club.
59. *The Houston Lawyer* 5.5 (May 1968), p. 5.
60. HBA Minutes, October 31, 1968.
61. *The Houston Post*, May 29, 1970.
62. *The Houston Post*, November 27, 1977.
63. *The Houston Lawyer*, Centennial Issue 8.6 (June 1971), pp. 19–20.
64. *The Houston Lawyer* 8.8 (August 1971), p. 5.
65. Hartford H. Prewett. Personal interview by James M. Riley, Jr. HBA Archives; *The Houston Lawyer* 8.12 (December 1971), p. 5.
66. HBA Minutes, October 30, 1971.
67. HBA Minutes, October 30, 1971.
68. HBA Minutes, April 1972.
69. The first member was David A. Simmons in 1944.
70. *The Houston Lawyer* 9.2 (February 1972), p. 5.

Chapter Six

1. Jerold S. Auerbach, *Unequal Justice: Lawyers and Social Change in Modern America* (New York: Oxford University Press, 1976), p. 7.

2. As quoted in Auerbach, p. 301. Auerbach cites "An Awful Lot of Lawyers Involved," *Time* (July 9, 1973).

3. *The Houston Lawyer* 10.9 (September 1973), p. 5.

4. *The Houston Lawyer* 11.9–10 (September–October 1974), p. 5.

5. *The Houston Lawyer* 11.11–12 (November–December 1974), p. 9.

6. *The Houston Lawyer* 19.2 (October 1981), p. 56; For Jaworski's personal account of the Watergate prosecution, see Leon Jaworski, *The Right and the Power: The Prosecution of Watergate* (Houston: Gulf Publishing Company, 1976).

7. The HBA held its first "legal clinics" in 1938 under the sponsorship of the Education Committee. This committee functioned as the coordinating and administrative organ of legal education until 1953, when it was replaced by the Lectures and Institutes Committee. In 1965, the Lectures and Institutes Committee became the Continuing Legal Education Committee, with institute and seminar sub-committees.

8. James B. Sales. Personal interview by Kerry Notestine, May 22, 1990. HBA Archives.

9. *The Houston Lawyer* 11.6 (June 1974), p. 9.

10. Justice Eugene A. Cook. Personal interview by Charles W. Giraud and Eric L. Fredrickson. December 14, 1990. HBA Archives.

11. James B. Sales interview; *The Houston Lawyer* 11.6 (June 1974), p. 6.

12. Griffin Smith, Jr., "Empires of Paper," *Texas Monthly* 1.10 (November 1973), pp. 54–55.

13. The traditional "Big Five" were Andrews & Kurth, Baker & Botts, Fulbright & Jaworski, Vinson & Elkins, and Butler & Binion.

14. Pearson Grimes. Statement during personal interview of Arthur P. Terrell. HBA Archives.

15. From "Submission of Houston Bar Association for Award of Merit Certificate of Achievement." HBA Archives.

16. Report of the Award of Merit Committee, 1975. HBA Archives.

17. *The Houston Lawyer* 12.1 (January 1975), p. 1.

18. *The Houston Lawyer* 12.9 (October 1975), p. 5.

19. Tom Arnold. Personal interview by Clinton F. Morse. December 13, 1986. HBA Archives.

20. *The Houston Lawyer* 16.4 (Summer 1979), p. 8.

21. *The Houston Lawyer* 18.3 (December 1980), p. 21.

22. "History of the Houston Bar Association." Unknown author, contained in the "HBA Resource and Reference Manual."

23. Dispute Resolution Centers Information Pamphlet.

24. *The Houston Lawyer* 19.1 (August 1981), p. 6.
25. *Houston Bar Bulletin* 81.11 (May 27, 1981).
26. Otway B. Denny, Jr. Personal letter to William K. Wilde, September 24, 1982.
27. Bates v. State Bar of Arizona, 433 U.S. 350 (1977).
28. Bates v. State Bar of Arizona, 433 U.S. 350 (1977).
29. Houston Bar Association Directory of Committees, 1980–81.
30. *The Houston Lawyer* 18.3 (December 1980), pp. 4–5.
31. *The Houston Lawyer* 19.1 (August 1981), p. 8; See also "Report of the Long-Range Planning and Development Committee to the Houston Bar Association Board of Directors, 1981." HBA Archives.
32. *Texas Bar Journal* 50.6 (June 1987).
33. Albert B. Kimball, Jr. Personal interview. HBA Archives.
34. The *Texas Lawyer* (June 30–July 4, 1986).
35. *The Houston Lawyer* 19.1 (August 1981), p. 5.
36. *The Houston Lawyer* 19.1 (August 1981), p. 5.
37. James B. Sales interview.
38. Frank B. Davis. Personal interview by Clinton F. Morse. HBA Archives.
39. Frank B. Davis. Personal interview by Clinton F. Morse. HBA Archives.
40. *The Houston Lawyer* 26.5 (March–April 1989), p. 6.
41. For the *Chronicle*'s position, see "Saturday Forum" for September 27, 1980; "Viewpoints," September 28, 1980; "Editorial: Ballot Shows Need for Change in Electing Judges," April 15, 1982; Nene Foxhall's article, "Method of Selecting Judges is on Collision Course with Politics," July 25, 1982; and Bo Boyers, "Sudden Spotlight on a Texas Judicial Problem," October 10, 1982.
42. *The Houston Lawyer* 20.3 (December 1982), p. 6.
43. *Houston Chronicle*, April 2, 1989.
44. *Houston Chronicle*, September 20, 1986.
45. *The Houston Lawyer* 26.3 (November–December 1988), p. 6.
46. *Houston Chronicle*, August 6, 1985.
47. The *Texas Lawyer* (December 11, 1985), p. 1.
48. The *Texas Lawyer* (December 11, 1985), p. 3.
49. The *Texas Lawyer* (December 11, 1985), p. 3.
50. *The Houston Lawyer* 23.1 (August 1985), pp. 6, 44.
51. National Association of Bar Executives Newsletter, Winter 1987.
52. *The Houston Post*, November 23, 1986.
53. *Houston Chronicle*, September 7, 1986.
54. *Houston Chronicle*, April 13, 1989.
55. Unidentified article in HBA "Publicity Received in 1987–1988" file. HBA Archives.
56. *Texas Bar Journal* 49.4 (April 1986), p. 413.

57. *The Houston Lawyer* 24.4 (January–February 1987), p. 35; National Association of Bar Executives Newsletter, Spring 1987.
58. As quoted in the *Houston Bar Bulletin* 89.3 (March 1989).
59. *The Houston Lawyer* 24.2 (September–October 1986).
60. Unidentified article in HBA "Publicity Received in 1987–1988" file. HBA Archives.
61. *Bar Leader* (March–April 1988), pp. 22–23.
62. *Houston Chronicle*, December 2, 1987.
63. *Houston Chronicle*, April 28, 1988; *The Houston Post*, April 30, 1988.
64. *The Houston Lawyer* 26.4 (January–February, 1989), p. 6; The legal profession has used the terms "Rambo" and "Ramboism" to describe the crisis in professionalism because they are synonymous with the machoism and toughness of the fictional movie character "Rambo" of the 1980s.
65. *The Houston Lawyer* 26.4 (January–February 1989), p. 6.
66. Justice Eugene A. Cook. Personal interview by Charles W. Giraud and Eric L. Fredrickson. December 14, 1990. HBA Archives.
67. *The Houston Lawyer* 25.1 (July–August 1987), p. 6.
68. *Houston Chronicle*, April 5, 1989.
69. Justice Eugene A. Cook interview.
70. For more details of this incident, see the *Houston Chronicle*, July 14, 1990.
71. *Houston Chronicle*, February 28, 1991.
72. Pearson Grimes. Personal interview by Eric L. Fredrickson. November 27, 1990. HBA Archives.
73. Based on a scientific survey of its members conducted by Rice University's Stephen Klineberg, the HBA "emphatically expressed its disapproval" of the partisan election of judges.
74. *The Houston Lawyer* 29.1 (July–August 1991), p. 6.

Epilogue

1. Justice Eugene A. Cook. Personal interview by Charles W. Giraud and Eric L. Fredrickson. December 14, 1990. HBA Archives.
2. *Texas Bar Journal* 51.8 (September 1988), p. 826.
3. Justice Eugene A. Cook interview.
4. Pearson Grimes. Personal interview conducted by Eric L. Fredrickson, November 27, 1990. HBA Archives.
5. Justice Eugene A. Cook interview; Grimes created a committee called "Minority Opportunities in the Profession."
6. Roland B. Voight, response to HBA's History Questionnaire, 1986. HBA Archives.
7. Pearson Grimes. Personal interview conducted by Eric L. Fredrickson, November 27, 1990. HBA Archives.
8. Justice Eugene A. Cook interview.

Bibliography

Unpublished Sources

Bracewell, Searcy. "Bracewell & Patterson: 'Some Early Recollections.'" Houston, Texas, 1981.

History of the Law Firm of Patterson, Boyd, Lowery & Aderholt. Courtesy of Ben L. Aderholt.

Houston Bar Association Archives, Houston, Texas.

Anderson, Doris E. Personal interview by Eric L. Fredrickson. March 30, 1990.

Arnold, Tom. Personal interview by Clinton F. Morse. December 13, 1986.

Barnett, W. Carroll, Jr. Houston Bar Association History Questionnaire. 1986.

Barrow, George T. Personal interview by Clinton F. Morse.

Bracewell, J.S. Papers.

Burg, Joyce. Personal interview by Eric L. Fredrickson. October 1, 1990.

Carothers, Durell M. Houston Bar Association History Questionnaire. 1986.

Cole, Robert L., Jr. Houston Bar Association History Questionnaire. 1986.

Cook, Justice Eugene A. Personal interview by Charles W. Giraud and Eric L. Fredrickson. December 14, 1990.

Davis, Frank B. Personal interview by Clinton F. Morse.

Denny, Otway B., Jr. Personal letter. September 24, 1982.

Eastland, Seaborn, Jr. Personal interview by Clinton F. Morse.

Finney, Barbara. Personal interview by Eric L. Fredrickson. March 30, 1990.

Grimes, Pearson. Personal interview by Eric L. Fredrickson. November 27, 1990.

"History of the Houston Bar Association." In *Houston Bar Association Resource and Reference Manual.*

"The History of the Women's Auxiliary to the Houston Bar Association." In *Women's Auxiliary to the Houston Bar Association 1986–1987 Yearbook.*

187

Houston Bar Association. *Annual Report.* 1985–86.

Houston Bar Association. *Bar Association Syllabus.* 1925.

Houston Bar Association. *Board of Directors' Minutes.* 1923–90.

Houston Bar Association. *Committee Books.* 1963–70.

Houston Bar Association. *Constitution and By-Laws.* 1936.

Houston Bar Association. *Directory.* 1939–41.

Houston Bar Association. *Directory of Committees.* 1980–81.

Houston Bar Association. *Houston Bar Bulletin.* 1941–63.

Houston Bar Association. *Houston Bar Journal.* 1931.

Houston Bar Association. *The Houston Lawyer.* 1963–91.

Houston Bar Association. *Pictorial Roster.* 1961–90.

Houston Bar Association. *Recommended Minimum Fee Schedule of the Houston Bar Association.* 1966.

Houston Bar Association. *Report of the President.* 1910, 1945, 1949, 1950, 1952.

Houston Bar Foundation. *Board of Directors' Minutes.* 1983–90.

Kennerly, T. Everton. Personal interview by Kerry E. Notestine. August 1987.

Kimball, Albert B. Personal interview by Jim Riley.

Kronzer, W. James. Personal interview by Clinton F. Morse and Eric L. Fredrickson. June 26, 1990.

McConn, Jack L. Personal interview by Charlotte C. Orr and Eric L. Fredrickson. November 19, 1990.

Parks, Fred. Personal interview by Eric L. Fredrickson. June 19, 1990.

Patterson, Harry W. Personal interview by Kerry E. Notestine. January 29, 1987.

Phillips, Thomas M. Personal interview by Joe Pratt. May 27, 1988.

Pletcher, George E. Personal interview by Jim Riley.

Pressler, Herman. Personal interview by Clinton F. Morse.

Prewett, Hartford H. Personal interview by Jim Riley.

Report of the Long-Range Planning and Development Committee to the Houston Bar Association Board of Directors. 1981.

Rouse, Mildred H. Personal interview by Eric L. Fredrickson. March 30, 1990.

Russell, Billye N. Houston Bar Association's History Questionnaire. 1986.

Sales, James B. Personal interview by Kerry E. Notestine. May 22, 1990.

Saunders, Charles. Telephone interview by Eric L. Fredrickson. January 11, 1991.

Tennant, Judge Geraldine B. Personal interview by Eric L. Fredrickson. March 30, 1990.

Timanus, Hall E. Personal interview by Clinton F. Morse.

Terrell, Arthur P. Houston Bar Association's History Questionnaire. 1986.

———. Personal interview by Pearson Grimes.

Walker, Judge Carl, Jr. Personal interview by Eric L. Fredrickson. July 24, 1990.

Westerfield, Nancy V. Personal interview by Eric L. Fredrickson. June 18, 1990.

Wilde, William Key. Personal interview by Kerry E. Notestine.

Houston Metropolitan Research Center, Houston, Texas.

Butler, George A. Personal interview by Thomas H. Kreneck and Louis Marchiafava. November 18, 1982.

Campbell, Ben S. Collection.

Connally, Ben C. Personal interview by Louis Marchiafava. April 2, 1975.

Harris County Law Library Catalog. 1949.

Hill, George A., Jr., Collection.

Houston Bar Association. *Annual Banquet Dinner Program.* 1906, 1908, 1909.

Houston Bar Association. *Constitution and By-Laws.* 1904.

Houston Bar Association. *Constitution and Roster.* 1929.

Houston Biography Scrapbook, Men. Vol. 16.

Houston Biography Scrapbook, Women. Vol. 17c.

Houston Law School Collection.

Roberts, Ingham. "Evolution of Harris County Courthouse." In *Ring Scrapbook*.

Merseburger, Marion. "A Political History of Houston, Texas, During the Reconstruction Period as Recorded by the Press: 1868–1873." Master's Thesis, Rice Institute, 1950.

Murray, Sean Collins. "Texas Prohibition Politics, 1887–1914." Master's Thesis, University of Houston, 1968.

Simmons, David A. *American Bar Association Annual Report, 1945.*

Streetman, Sam. Letter to Jesse H. Jones. June 25, 1932. Andrews & Kurth Archives.

Published Sources

Agnew, Lea and Jo Ann Haden-Miller. *Atlanta and Its Lawyers: A Century of Vision, 1888–1988.* Atlanta: Atlanta Bar Association, 1988.

Alexander, Charles C. "Crusade for Conformity: The Ku Klux Klan in Texas, 1920–1930." *Texas Gulf Coast Historical Association* 6.1 (August 1962).

——— . *The Ku Klux Klan in the Southwest.* Lexington: University of Kentucky Press, 1965.

Andrews, Jesse. "A Texas Portrait: Captain James A. Baker, 1857–1941." *Texas Bar Journal* (February 1961), pp. 110–111; 187–189.

Application of Levy. 214 *Federal Reporter* 2d 331 (5th Cir. 1954), *rev'd per curiam,* 348 *United States Reports* 978 (1955).

Auerbach, Jerold. *Unequal Justice: Lawyers and Social Change in Modern America.* New York: Oxford University Press, 1976.

Austin, Stephen F. *The Austin Papers.* 3 Vols. Eugene C. Barker, ed. Washington, D.C.: U.S. Government Printing Office, 1928.

Baines, Mrs. W. M., ed. *Houston's Part in the World War.* Houston: Houston Chamber of Commerce, 1919.

Baker, Botts in World War II: A Collection of Narrative Accounts of their Service Experiences. North River Press, 1947.

Ball, Colonel Thomas H. *The Port of Houston: How it Came to Pass.* Houston: reprinted from articles appearing in the Houston Chronicle and Houston Post, August 2–November 1, 1936.

Bates v. State Bar of Arizona. 433 *United States Reports* 350 (1977).

Beard, Norman H., ed. *The Municipal Book of the City of Houston, 1922.* Houston, 1922.

Big Town, Big Money: The Business of Houston. Houston: Cordovan Press, 1973.

Biographical Encyclopedia of Texas. New York: Southern Publishing Company, 1880.

Bloomfield, Maxwell. "The Texas Bar in the Nineteenth Century." *Vanderbilt Law Review* 32.1 (1979), pp. 261–276.

Bodenhamer, David J., and James W. Ely, Jr. eds. *Ambivalent Legacy: A Legal History of the South.* Jackson: University Press of Mississippi, 1984.

Bowner, Jim D. "The Presidents." In *Centennial History of the Texas Bar, 1881–1982.* Burnet, Texas: Eakin Press, 1981.

Buenger, Walter L. and Joseph A. Pratt. *But Also Good Business: Texas Commerce Banks and the Financing of Houston and Texas, 1886–1986.* College Station: Texas A & M University Press, 1986.

Burney, Cecil E. "Texas Bar Acts on Legal Aid: 'Equal Justice Under Law.'" *American Bar Association Journal* 38 (May 1952), pp. 396–397.

Carleton, Don E. *Red Scare! Right-Wing Hysteria, Fifties Fanaticism and their Legacy in Texas.* Austin: Texas Monthly Press, 1985.

Carroll, B. H. "The Bench and Bar." *Standard History of Houston, Texas.* Knoxville: H.W. Crew, 1912.

The City of Houston, and Harris County, Texas. The World's Columbian Exposition Souvenir. Houston: Post Engraving Company, 1893.

Committee on History and Tradition of the State Bar of Texas. *Centennial History of the Texas Bar, 1882–1982.* Burnet: Eakin Press, 1981.

Daniels, Pat A. *Texas Avenue at Main Street: The Chronological Story of a City Block in Houston, The Most Significant Block in the History of Texas.* Houston: Allen Press, 1964.

Davidson, Chandler. "Houston: The City Where the Business of Government is Business." In *Public Policy in Texas.* Wendall Bedichek and Neal Tannhill, eds. New York: Scott Foresman, 1982.

Davis, Michael R. "A History of the Houston Law School." *The Houston Lawyer* 15.2 (Summer 1978), pp. 26–41; *ibid.* 16.1 (Fall 1978), pp. 30–38.

Dugas, Vera L. "A Duel with Railroads: Houston vs. Galveston, 1866–1881." *East Texas Historical Journal* 2.2 (October 1964), pp. 118–127.

Dwyer, Frances Craighead. "The Development of the Legal Aid Movement in the Southeast." *Tennessee Law Review* 22 (1951–53), pp. 497–501.

The Encyclopedia of the New West. Marshall, Texas, 1881.

Feagin, Joe R. *Free Enterprise City: Houston in Political and Economic Perspective.* London: Rutgers University Press, 1988.

Fletcher, Herbert, ed. *Harris County: Republic of Texas, 1839–45.* Houston: Anson Jones Press, 1950.

40 *Texas Reports* (1874)

Friedman, Lawrence M. *A History of American Law, 2nd ed.* New York: Simon and Schuster, 1985.

Fuermann, George M. "Notes and Documents: Houston, 1880–1910." *Southwestern Historical Quarterly* 71.2 (October 1967), pp. 227–242.

Galveston Daily News.

Garwood, H.M. "History of the Houston Bench and Bar." *The New Encyclopedia of Texas*, 1926, pp. 43–45.

Gawalt, Gerald, ed. *The New High Priests: Lawyers in Post-Civil War America.* Westport, Conn., 1984.

Gideon v. Wainwright. 372 United States Reports 335 (1963).

Gilmer, Daffan. "Early Courts and Lawyers of Texas." *Texas Law Review* 12 (June 1934), pp. 435–52.

Gray, William Fairfax. *From Virginia to Texas, 1835, Diary of Col. Wm. F. Gray.* Houston, 1965.

Greene, Casey. "Guardians Against Change: The Ku Klux Klan in Houston and Harris County, 1920–1925." *Houston Review* 10.1 (1988), pp. 3–20.

Gresham, Newton. "The Houston Bar, 1930's & 1940's." *The Houston Lawyer* 16.2 (Winter 1978).

Gruben, Karl T. and James E. Hambleton. *A Reference Guide to Texas Law and Legal History, 2nd ed.*, 1987.

Hall, Kermit L. *The Magic Mirror: Law in American History.* New York: Oxford University Press, 1989.

Harris, Dilue. "Reminiscences of Mrs. Dilue Harris." In *Houston: A Nation's Capital, 1837–1839.* Edited by the Harris County Historical Society. Houston: D. Armstrong Co., 1985, pp. 39–42.

Haynes, Robert V. *A Night of Violence: the Houston Riot of 1917.* Baton Rouge: Louisiana State University Press, 1976.

Herndon, John H. "A Diary of a Young Man." In *Houston: A Nation's Capital, 1837–1839.* Edited by the Harris County Historical Society. Houston: D. Armstrong Co., 1985, pp. 79–90.

History of Texas with a Biographical History of the Cities of Houston and Galveston. Chicago: Lewis Publishing Co., 1895.

Hobson, Wayne K. "Symbol of the New Profession: Emergence of the Large Law Firm, 1870–1915." In *The New High Priests: Lawyers in Post-Civil War America*, Gerald W. Gawalt, ed. Westport: Greenwood Press, 1984, pp. 3–22.

——— · *The American Legal Profession and the Organizational Society, 1890–1930.* New York: Garland Publishing, 1986.

Houston (Chamber of Commerce Magazine).

Houston: A History and Guide. Houston: The Anson Jones Press, 1942.

Houston Chronicle.

Houston City Directory.

The Houston Post (known variously as *Houston Post, Houston Daily Post, Daily Post, Houston Post-Dispatch*).

Houston Press.

Houston Press Club. *Men of Affairs and Representative Institutions of Houston and Environs.* Houston, 1913.

Houston Telegraph.

Huber, Stephen K., and James E. Myers. "Admission to the Practice of Law in Texas: An Analytical History." Houston Law Review 15.3 (March 1978), pp. 485–533.

Hurst, Willard J. *The Growth of American Law: The Law Makers.* Boston: Little, Brown and Company, 1950.

Hutcheson, Palmer. "Earliest Effort to Secure 25 foot Channel Described." *Houston* 8 (November 1937), pp. 3–4.

Jaworski, Leon. *After Fifteen Years.* Houston: Gulf Publishing, 1961.

——— · *The Right and the Power: The Prosecution of Watergate.* Houston: Gulf Publishing Company, 1976.

Jaworski, Leon, with Mickey Herskowitz. *Confession and Avoidance: A Memoir.* Garden City, New York: Anchor Press/Doubleday, 1979.

Johnson, Earl, Jr. *Justice and Reform: The Formative Years of the OEO Legal Services Program.* New York: Russell Sage Foundation, 1974.

Kelly, Hugh Rice. "Peter Gray." *The Houston Lawyer* 13.1 (January 1976), pp. 29–34.

Kittrell, Norman G. *Governors Who Have Been, and Other Public Men of Texas.* Houston, 1921.

Kogan, Herman. *The First Century: The Chicago Bar Association, 1874–1974.* Chicago: Rand McNally, 1974.

Lasswell, Mary. *John Henry Kirby: Prince of the Pines.* Austin: Encino Press, 1967.

"Legal Aid Committees and Agencies." In *The Martindale-Hubbell Law Directory.* New York: Martindale-Hubbell, 1940–1948.

Lipartito, Kenneth, and Joseph Pratt. *Baker & Botts in the Development of Modern Houston.* Austin: University of Texas Press, 1991.

Lynch, James D. *The Bench and Bar of Texas.* St. Louis, 1885.

Martin, George. *Causes and Conflicts: The Centennial History of the Association of the Bar of the City of New York, 1870–1970.* Boston: Houghton Mifflin Company, 1970.

McAshan, Marie Phelps. *On the Corner of Main and Texas: A Houston Legacy.* Houston: Hutchins House, distributed by Gulf Publishing Co., 1985.

McComb, David G. *Houston: The Bayou City.* Austin: University of Texas Press, 1969.

Meiners, Fredericka. *A History of Rice University: The Institute Years, 1907–1963.* Houston: Rice University Studies, 1982.

Meserve, Robert W. *The American Bar Association: A Brief History and Appreciation.* New York: The Newcomen Society, 1973.

Morello, Karen Berger. *The Invisible Bar: The Woman Lawyer in America 1638 to the Present.* Boston: Beacon Press, 1986.

Muir, Andrew Forest. "Algernon P. Thompson." *Southwestern Historical Quarterly* 51.2 (October 1947), pp. 143–149.

———. "Augustus M. Tomkins, Frontier Prosecutor." *Southwestern Historical Quarterly* 54.3 (January 1951), pp. 316–323.

———. "Murder on Madison Avenue." *William Marsh Rice and His Institute: A Biographical Study.* Sylvia Stallings Morris, ed. Houston: Rice University Studies, 1972.

——— · *Texas in 1837: An Anonymous, Contemporary Narrative.* Austin: University of Texas Press, 1958.

New Encyclopedia of Texas. Dallas: Texas Development Bureau, 1925.

O'Connor, Michol and J. W. Johnson. "Harris County Courthouse: Some Historical Notes." *The Houston Lawyer* 12.10 (November 1975), pp. 40–49.

Phillips, Thomas M. "The Houston Plan: An Overview." *Texas Bar Journal* (October 1966), pp. 819–821.

Platt, Harold. *City Building in the New South: The Growth of Public Services in Houston, Texas, 1830–1910.* Philadelphia: Temple University Press, 1983.

Potts, Charles S. "Early Criminal Law in Texas: From Civil Law to Common Law, to Code." *Texas Law Review* 21 (April 1943), pp. 394–406.

Pound, Roscoe. *The Lawyer from Antiquity to Modern Times.* St. Paul, Minn.: West Publishing Company, 1953.

Proceedings of the Texas Bar Association, 1882–1938.

Redford, David C. "The Houston Junior Bar Association: Its Past, Present, and Future." *The Houston Lawyer* 7.12 (December 1970), pp. 7–21.

"Report of the Committee on Legal Aid Work." In *Annual Report of the American Bar Association.* Chicago: American Bar Association, 1921–1950.

Report of the Committee on Legal Education and Admission to the Bar. "Legal Education and Admission to the Bar." *Texas Bar Journal* 1.7 (July 1938), pp. 196–199.

"Report of the Standing Committee on Legal Aid Work." *Annual Report of the American Bar Association* 75 (Chicago: ABA, 1950), p. 472.

Rippe, Peter M. "Other Landmarks of History." *The Houston Lawyer* 13.2 (February 1976), pp. 38–43.

Roberts, O. M. "Legal Education and Admissions to the Bar." In *Proceedings of the Third Annual Session of the Texas Bar Association,* 1884, pp. 43–48.

Rotenberg, Daniel L., ed. "Legal Services for the Poor—Houston: An Analysis of the Houston Legal Foundation, An OEO Funded Legal Services Program." *Houston Law Review* 6.5 (May 1969).

Scruggs v. Houston Legal Foundation. 475 *Southwestern Reporter* 2d 604 (Tex. Civ. App.—Houston [1st Dist.] 1972, no writ).

Sheppard, Anthony. "The Nineteenth Century Bench and Bar in Harris County, Texas." *The Houston Lawyer* 13.5 (July 1976), pp. 6–14.

Sibley, Marilyn McAdams. *The Port of Houston: A History.* Austin: University of Texas Press, 1968.

Smith, Griffin, Jr. "Empires of Paper." *Texas Monthly* 1.10 (November 1973).

Smith, Reginald H. *Justice and the Poor.* New York: Carnegie Foundation, 1919.

———. "Legal Aid During the War and After." *American Bar Association Journal* 31 (January 1945), pp. 18–21.

The Standard Blue Book of Texas—Edition De Luxe of Houston. Houston: Who's Who Publishing Company, 1907.

Steiner, Mark E. "'If We Don't Do Anything But Have an Annual Dinner': The Early History of the Houston Bar Association." *Houston Review* 11.2 (1989), pp. 95–110.

Stottlemire, Marvin. "Chronology: November 29, 1870–May 21, 1971." *The Houston Lawyer* (June 1971).

Telegraph and Texas Register.

Texas Bar Journal.

The Texas Lawyer.

Touchy v. Houston Legal Foundation. 417 *Southwestern Reporter* 2d 625 (Tex. Civ. App.—Waco 1967) *rev'd*, 432 S.W. 2d 690 (Tex. 1968).

Tucker, Leah Brooke. "The First Administration of Mayor Lewis Cutrer of Houston, 1958–1960." *East Texas Historical Journal* 12.1 (Spring 1974).

U.S. Bureau of the Census.

Wiebe, Robert H. *The Search for Order, 1877–1920.* New York: Hill & Wang, 1967.

Wood, W. D. "Reminiscences of Texas and Texans Fifty Years Ago." *The Quarterly of the Texas State Historical Association* 5.2 (October 1901).

Yarborough, Ralph W. "A History of Law Licensing in Texas." In *Centennial History of the Texas Bar, 1882–1982*, 1981, pp. 181–193.

Young, S. O. *A Thumb-Nail History of Houston, Texas.* Houston: Rein & Sons Co., 1912.

———. *True Stories of Old Houston and Houstonians: Historical and Personal Sketches.* Galveston: Oscar Springer, 1913.

Index

* Boldface numbers indicate photographs.